IMPROVISING
JAZZ
BASS

By Richard Laird

Consolidated Music Publishers
New York • London • Sydney • Tokyo • Cologne

To L. Ron Hubbard, whose study technology has been of great assistance in the writing of this book.

Acknowledgements

Many thanks to Jason Shulman, David Katzenberg, Cameron Brown, and Billy Mintz for valuable ideas and opinions. And to all the many fine musicians it has been my good fortune to be associated with, a special thank you.

Note: The author welcomes any communication regarding this book. Address correspondence to: Rick Laird, c/o Consolidated Music Publishers, 33 West 60th Street, New York, New York 10023.

e d c b a

International Standard Book Number: 0-8256-4091-1
Library of Congress Catalog Card Number: 79-54366

Distributed throughout the world by Music Sales Corporation:

33 West 60th Street, New York 10023
78 Newman Street, London W1P 3LA
4-26-22 Jingumae, Shibuya-ku, Tokyo 150
27 Clarendon Street, Artarmon, Sydney NSW 2064
Kölner Strasse 199, D-5000, Cologne 90

Contents

Preface

The purpose of this book is to provide the aspiring bassist with data vital to performing successfully in a wide variety of contemporary musical situations. More specifically, it is designed to help in those situations where a notated bass part is not provided, and where it is the bassist's responsibility to create or improvise a part appropriate to the music at hand.

The ability to do this well rests largely on the individual's knowledge of the harmonic material within the musical idiom that he or she wants to play, plus skill in applying this knowledge directly to the instrument.

Since the melodic, harmonic, and rhythmic structure of a piece of music relies heavily on the bass to give it its foundation, the bass player must take his or her role in this responsibility seriously. Just as a building built on a weak foundation will soon collapse, a piece of music being performed by a group with an unsure bassist is liable to fall apart. A large percentage of contemporary music—both jazz and pop—features the bass more than ever before, and the bassist is required to lay down his part in a positive and forthright manner, with certainty and conviction. These are some of the key ingredients in playing the role of bassist well. One thing is certain—guessing does not work.

The information collected in this book is designed to assist the student who is eager to overcome his confusion, and eliminate whatever guesswork he relies on in attempting to fill this role. There is nothing radically new about this information—it has been around for a long time and is common knowledge among the majority of skilled musicians. What is new is the presentation of this information in a clear and precise form especially for the bassist.

Since this book deals with *what* to play rather than *how* to play, discussions or explanations of instrumental and musical basics have been avoided. The exercises and ideas presented here can be easily applied by the student who has some knowledge of the bass and the rudiments of music. An excellent book to use as a guide to obtaining basic music skills is *Elementary Training for Musicians*, by Paul Hindemith. This or a similar book on the subject should be kept handy while studying so that any misunderstandings that arise can be cleared up.

To be a creative, well-rounded bassist is a worthy goal, and if this book serves in some small way to aid the student on his or her journey, my purpose will be fulfilled.

About the Bass and Bass Players

Bass guitar first appeared on the music scene in the early 1950s. The most popular model at that time was the Fender Bass, created by Leo Fender. As rock music began to develop, bass guitar gradually began to replace its predecessor, the acoustic bass. This was largely due to the volume of the music and the difficulty at that time of amplifying the acoustic. By the late 1950s it became evident that bass guitar was well on its way to becoming a bona fide musical instrument in its own right, and with the advent of 1960s rock music it was clear that it had arrived to stay. Since then, it has become an integral part of virtually every rock and pop group and its sound is heard on the majority of records made today.

However, its use in jazz is relatively recent. Since the mid-sixties many acoustic players began to double on bass guitar as the demands of the music changed. Some abandoned acoustic entirely.

There are many different points of view about the use of bass guitar in jazz, both pro and con. The most prevalent point of view (and the one with which I agree), is that nothing will ever replace the quality, texture, and beauty of the acoustic bass. In the hands of a skilled player, it is a magnificent sound to behold. To compare the quality of the two instruments is rather pointless. It's a little like comparing a horse to a donkey: They are different animals, although they can have similar form and function. What, then, is the position of bass guitar in jazz? Wide open! With the arrival on the music scene of players such as Jaco Pastorius with Weather Report and Stanley Clarke with Return to Forever and other adventurous souls, it is clear that possibilities exist to play beyond the endlessly repeated root-fifth "vamps" syndrome most commonly associated with the instrument. As more and more young players emerge from rock/pop groups, eager to expand their musical horizons, it is only a matter of time until there will be many fine players making meaningful contributions to the ever expanding field of contemporary jazz.

Since the concept of jazz bass evolved from a long line of acoustic bassists, it would be folly for the earnest student to ignore the work of these fine artists who paved the way. To this end I have included at the end of this book a list of key figures who have had, and continue to have, a major influence on the development of a creative bass style. I strongly urge the student to track down recordings of these artists as the music speaks far more eloquently on the subject than any textbook could hope to.

Finally, to repeat what I said earlier, the possibilities for creating meaningful music on bass guitar are wide open. There are absolutely no limitations save the ones that you create for yourself! With faith, persistence and work you will achieve your goal. It's a great game, enjoy it!

Purchasing Bass Equipment

The Fender bass has long been considered the norm in bass guitar. However, there are now so many different models that it would be difficult to list them all. Basically, your choice of instrument is a matter of personal taste and budget. Prices vary greatly. The early model Fenders (pre-CBS) can cost three or four times that of a new bass. Generally, the most expensive basses are the custom designed models, such as Alembic, Carl Thompson, etc.

One does not, however, need to spend a large amount of money for an instrument that plays and sounds good. A $2,500 bass in the hands of an inept player will not sound better than a $200 bass played by an inspired musician.

The qualities to look for when buying an instrument are as follows:

Sound Quality

—Listen for an evenness of tone up and down the neck on each string.

—Note the type of pickup or pickups used.

—Check for a good range of treble and bass tone variations.

—There should be an overall clarity of sound free of distortion.

Neck and Fingerboard

—Examine the straightness of the neck and mark the type of truss rod used to adjust it.

—Note the thickness of the neck: Does it suit the size of your hand?

—Find out what type of wood is used on the fingerboard. Generally rosewood or other hardwood is preferable because its density gives a better quality sound.

Action

—Does it feel easy, stiff, too high, or too low? There should be no string noise or rattle on any fret for all four strings.

—Most basses have adjustment controls to raise or lower the strings set on the tailpiece. Are these controls easily accessible?

General Intonation

—Always check to see how true the pitch is, especially at the top of the neck.

—Most basses have ways of adjusting the intonation of individual strings down by the bridge. Check the accuracy and design of these controls.

—Examine the design of the machine heads. Are they sturdy, or prone to slip? Once a note is brought up to pitch, it should stay in pitch—if it slips, it may be a faulty machine head.

Overall Reliability

—Is the instrument built to last, and will it survive under rigorous conditions? A pretty bass will be a liability if the neck is prone to warping, snapping, or other disasters.

These are the main things to look for when buying an instrument. It is wise to try several before you decide. Don't be duped by high pressure salesmen into buying a bass that you're not totally happy with. If you're unsure, bring someone with you who knows what to look for. Your personal "sound" is by far your biggest asset, and a good instrument can give you pleasure for many years.

Fretted or Fretless?

The majority of bassists use fretted instruments. However, fretless bass is becoming quite popular and offers a wider range of expression than fretted bass. The overall sound quality is different, and one is provided with a comparatively better sustain. The absence of frets allows for a certain amount of creative play with intonation, and gives the musician the option to use various technical devices such as vibrato, or sliding up or down when approaching a note. Fretless bass is, for these reasons, more difficult to play and the majority of recording bassists use a fretted instrument as intonation must be spot-on in the studio. It can be difficult to sightread a bass part on fretless bass—one must concentrate on the part plus keep the pitch of each note accurate. Personally, I use a fretted bass for recording and a fretless (Fender *Jazz Bass*) for more adventurous situations where it seems appropriate.

Strings

There are dozens of brands of strings on the market—some very good, and some very bad. Basically, there are four kinds: Flat wound, round wound, half round, and nylon tape. These are available in heavy, medium, or light gauge. The majority of studio bassists use flat wound strings as round wounds produce

a certain amount of "finger noise" not too popular with recording engineers. The round wounds do sound very good though, and many players who work in mostly clubs or live concerts use them for their brightness.

The choice of gauge or thickness is a matter of personal taste. While heavy gauge strings sound very good, on some instruments they can cause the neck to warp—making the action higher and throwing the tuning out. Medium and light gauge strings work well on most basses.

It's wise to experiment with several kinds of strings until you find a set that suits your instrument and style of playing. It pays to get the best that you can—strings are a crucial part of the sound quality that you produce.

Amplifiers

Again, there are many makes and types of amplifiers on the market. An amplifier is the terminal point of what you are playing on an instrument; it does, in fact, define your musical voice. Therefore it is important to select one that suits your style of playing and the musical situations that you will be involved with.

The things to look for when buying an amplifier are as follows:

Sound Quality

—Listen for a clear, distortion-free sound.

—See if it is a tube or transistor type amplifier.

—Note the range of variations that you can get from the tone control: Is there a good treble, middle, and bass?

Practicality of Size

—Make sure that the external workmanship is good.

—Ask yourself if it looks as though it will keep on working under rigorous conditions. An amplifier that breaks down frequently is a real liability to you and the group, and can cost money in cancelled engagements, repairs, etc. Have it thoroughly checked before purchasing, and keep the warranty!

Equipment Cases

Most basses come with a hard case, and for general purposes these will suffice. However, there are soft, form-fitting cases called "gig bags" which are less bulky for 'round-town use. One can also usually carry them onto planes and save any risk of damage.

For extensive travel situations, a good custom made heavy case lined with foam rubber is the best choice. This will protect the instrument from severe bumps and drops. They are expensive but a good investment in the long run. Similar cases for amplifiers can be found.

Equipment Care

It pays to keep your equipment in top condition so as to alleviate breakdowns on the job. Have the amplifier checked regularly.

Strings should be changed after they become "dead" harmonically. How often differs according to the frequency of use. Keep the neck and fingerboard clean—this will aid your playing facility.

Fundamentals of Technique

Positioning the Bass

In order to be comfortable while playing, it is important to position the bass next to the body in such a way as to have easy access to the entire fingerboard. Ideally it should remain at a 45-degree angle.

While it is not the rule, most bass players stand when performing, so it is necessary to adjust the bass strap until a comfortable position is found. A common problem with some basses is that the neck keeps moving downward and requires continual adjustment. One way to keep the balance between the neck and the body of the instrument in proper proportion, is to move the strap lug below the tailpiece a few inches to the left, when facing the front of the bass.

A good sturdy strap is a good asset and make sure that it is secure on the lugs. I had one slip off once during a concert—the neck hit the floor and snapped in half!

Positioning the Left Hand

A common error in faulty technique can be found in the manner in which the bassist uses his left hand. Many beginners use the "bunch-of-bananas" method—with the fingers cramped together and the thumb wrapped around the neck onto the fingerboard. While this may suffice for more simple forms of music, it can be a real hindrance in developing a fluid and articulate technique.

Positioning the Right Hand

The right hand is positioned in such a way as to provide easy access to the area of attack; i.e., the manner in which the strings are struck.

A variety of sounds can be created by attacking the strings in different places. Playing close to the end of the fingerboard produces a warm, mellow sound; playing above the pickup produces a bright type of sound; while playing down by the tailpiece will give you a harder, more percussive sound.

Right-Hand Techniques

There are two basic right-hand techniques that can be used for producing a sound from the strings: using the first and second fingers, or using a pick. For either alternative, aim to keep the right hand very relaxed at the wrist. This will increase your dexterity and ability to play for long periods of time without tiring.

While the majority of players seem to favor the two-finger style, the use of a pick is quite common among studio bass players as it produces a clear, bright sound which records well. Mastering this style is a study on its own, and is markedly different from the variety of techniques available from using the fingers alone.

The following is a list of different approaches to using the two-finger style:

—Alternating between the first and second fingers and plucking the strings upwards.

—Striking downward with the thumb while resting the other fingers on the body below the strings.

—Plucking two or more notes with the thumb, first, and second fingers—in the style of a classical guitarist.

—Using the thumb and first finger to pull a string off the fingerboard, and creating a percussive, snapping sound.

The student is urged to experiment with the various methods in order to find the one or more sounds that will suit (a) his style of playing, (b) the particular instrument being played, (c) the amplifier, and (d) individual taste.

About the Acoustic Bass

Acoustic bass is the largest instrument in the string family. Its use in jazz began with the first Dixieland bands when it began to replace the tuba. The first bassist to emerge as a real "voice" on the instrument was Jimmy Blanton who performed in the early Duke Ellington orchestras.

The study of acoustic bass is a subject in its own right. Since there are many excellent books covering this, the technical aspects of playing acoustic bass will not be dealt with here in order to concentrate on the improvisational aspects of the instrument.

By far the best way to develop a correct technique on acoustic bass is to find a good classical player who teaches. The fingering and bowing of the instrument are subjects that need to be carefully tutored in order to avoid forming incorrect playing habits at the early stage of development. The use of acoustic bass in contemporary popular music has declined somewhat since the mid-sixties, when Fender bass began to emerge. However, with the advent of better pickups and amplifiers for the instrument, the initial problem of producing a sufficient volume has largely been overcome and it is possible for an acoustic bassist to be heard clearly in a relatively loud group.

The leading jazz bassists in the field today generally have prodigious techniques. Many play solo lines equal to the best jazz guitarists. Eddie Gomez, Stanley Clarke, Mike Richmond, or Chuck Dominico are good examples of this new trend. While the bass guitar lends itself very well to percussive/rhythmic music; the acoustic bass definitely has the edge in terms of its quality of tone, sustain, depth of sound, and overall blend with other instruments in the jazz idiom. As a solo instrument, it can be used for a wider range of musical expression in that it can be bowed.

While it is fine to specialize in either electric or acoustic bass, the ideal for many players is to play both, and play them well. Acoustic bass is by far the most demanding of the two in that one must practice and play it constantly in order to keep up one's technique and maintain the physical stamina needed to produce a sound.

Buying an Acoustic Bass

The best advice I can offer for a new student interested in finding a good acoustic bass is to have a bass player or bass teacher help you. Music instrument stores generally do not carry acoustic basses and when they do they are usually of an inferior quality. Acoustic basses are not mass produced as are Fender basses. The majority of good sounding basses are at least fifty to one hundred years old and come from Italy, Germany, France, and England. Good American made acoustic basses are rare.

Most basses come in two sizes: 3/4 size and full size, with either a flat or a round back. Since each acoustic bass is unique in itself it is difficult to generalize as to which type sounds best. Full-size basses do not always have a bigger sound or a better tone, and they can be a hassle to transport. The following is a list of ways to find a good acoustic bass.

—Check with violin/bass repair shops.

—Get in touch with some professional bassists; they could be either jazz or symphony players. They often have several instruments, or they may know of a good one for sale.

—Place an ad in your local newspaper. This can sometimes produce good results as someone may have an old bass in the attic which can be bought for a bargain price. Usually these need major repair work, which is expensive: but considering the savings on the purchase price, it can turn out to be a very good investment. For example, I bought my current bass in London, England, for $100. It was in disastrous condition. I have spent to date about $800 on it and now have an excellent instrument worth much more than I invested.

Regardless of the way you intend to look for a bass, it is a good idea to have the opinion of a professional player or teacher before making the sale final. There are many pitfalls, and they can be costly. A more seasoned player can also advise you as to your choice of bow (French or German), the best type of strings, etc.

Acoustic-Bass Pickups

There are several bass pickups available on the market at this time. The most popular brands are *Underwood*, *Barcus-Berry*, and *Polytone*. Having tested all three, I personally like the Underwood bass pickup the best as it produces the most natural sound. However, many bassists get good results with the other two listed. Underwood pickups are available from Underwood Bass Pickups, P.O. Box 303, Carmel Valley, CA 93924. They cost at this time around one hundred dollars, and they need to be fitted to the bridge of the instrument by a bass repair craftsman.

Amplifiers for Acoustic Bass

The same principles that apply for electric bass amplifiers also apply here. The actual situation one is going to play in determines the type of amplifier needed. The Ampeg *B-15* is small, and works well for most 'round-town gigs. For concert and touring situations, where high volume is required, a larger amplfier may be needed. There are often problems with feedback: The tolerance for extremes in volume in all of the pickups that I listed is fairly low. It is best, when a lot of volume is required, to stand off to the side of the amplifier. This will cut down on the chance of feedback. I currently use, in combination with the Underwood pickup, the Polytone *Mini-Brute*. It comes with either a 12-inch or a 15-inch speaker. I find the 12-inch model ideal: It has sufficient power and volume for most playing situations plus it is very small, lightweight, and easy to transport. They are available from most large musical instrument stores and are reasonably priced.

Acoustic-Bass Care

Acoustic basses are rather fragile creatures and do not respond well to careless handling; like being kicked, dropped, or bumped against. Bass repairs are very costly, so pay close attention when transporting it to see that it doesn't get bumped or otherwise abused. Also, like humans, they do not like to be left alone for too long and thrive on affection. Treat your bass well and play it a lot, especially with the bow. This will help to keep the sound "alive."

When touring, it is best to take the bass on the plane and put it on the seat next to you where you can keep your eye on it. *Never* put it in baggage unless it's in a custom made fiberglass case. *Never* allow anyone to move it or carry it who is not experienced in handling basses. Most airlines charge full fare for the extra seat, but it is worth it for the peace of mind. In general, treat your bass well and it will treat you well for a long time.

About Bassists

Qualities to Aim For

Having listened to and observed many fine acoustic and electric bassists in the field of contemporary music, it comes to my attention that they have many qualities in common. The following list will give you some ideas of what to aim for.

Presence
The "thereness" and ability to project to an audience.

Quality and Clarity of Sound

Rhythmic Certainty
The ability to play *with* the group and hold it together while maintaining a steady and swinging flow or pulse.

Harmonic Skill
The capacity to create musical and interesting bass lines behind a soloist or ensemble. This inventiveness should be present in bass solos.

Technique
Adequate technical skill to convey the music precisely.

Reading Skills
A way to realize the composer's intentions quickly and accurately.

Inspiration
The ability to perform with "fire" and in an uplifting way—to inspire both the group and the audience.

Listening
The ability to "hear" and duplicate what's going on in the music and to act in a way that complements it.

Flexibility
The willingness to try something in different ways and be open to new ideas.

Lack of Seriousness
Have fun onstage, laugh at oneself and with others. Make light of things and generally be joyful while performing.

About Practicing

One of the most important and potentially rewarding areas in being a musician is the ability to practice correctly. In the course of teaching bass students over the past few years, it became clear to me that very few of these students knew how to practice, what to practice, or how to apply what they practiced to their professional situations. This chapter is devoted to taking a look at some approaches to practicing and how to get the most benefit from this activity.

Of all the musicians you will listen to in your life (assuming that you have decided or are deciding if you should be a full-time musician), there is no one musician's playing that you will be more familiar with than your own. This being the case, it follows that if you don't like what you're hearing in your own playing, it's going to be pretty difficult to project a positive, confident attitude to those that you are playing with. Remember that a large part of being a bassist is interacting with others.

So, the thing to do about this is to take a look at your playing in an objective way:
—Find out what your strong points are. What are the things that come naturally for you without much effort?
—Find out what your weak points are. What are the things that you struggle with and put a *lot* of effort into?

Make two lists on a sheet of paper. On one list, write out what you consider to be your strong points. On the second list, write out what you consider your weak points. Be very specific in this! Here is a mocked up example:

Strong Points	Weak Points
Good sound	Insufficient knowledge of
Sufficient technique	harmony and correct
Good ideas	notes to play on chords
Flexibility with others in	Poor reading skills
group	Poor rhythmic concept
Good "ears"	Confusion with fingering
	when playing certain
	scales

. . . and so on. Your lists, of course, will be based on your own insights. Only you can really know your strong and weak points and only you can be responsible for them.

Bear in mind that even the very best players have weak points—I have yet to encounter the absolutely "perfect" bassist. The idea is to take what you do well naturally and add to it by practicing those things that are difficult for you. No one is born with the ability to read music well. It is a developed skill and the way to get to be a good reader is simply to do it!

The way to begin is at the beginning. Learn the rudiments of music from a book or a teacher. Take it slowly, step by step, and go systematically to more difficult types of reading problems. Don't skip over things you don't understand thoroughly: Go back to the point where you did understand and find out specifically where the misconception occurred. Clear that up first.

It is important at this point to take a look at things objectively and find answers to the following questions:

—What is the existing condition of your musical abilities?

—What is your ideal condition for your musical abilities?

—What are your actual purposes and goals in this activity?

—What are your plans to achieve these goals?

—What can you actually do on a day-to-day basis to reach your ideal condition?

It is very important to answer these questions for yourself as it is very difficult to move towards a goal unless that goal is clearly defined. It is a good idea to keep a record of your progress and the actions taken day by day so as to know that you are reaching your goal.

It is helpful in determining the goals that you aspire to, to inspect the work of those bassists who have already made their mark and who continue to grow and expand in their field. In observing these players, try to define for yourself the various qualities they have acquired which keep them at the top of their field.

—Does listening and/or watching them perform excite you? Does it make you feel inspired, expansive, joyful?

—What quality in the way they communicate their music do you admire most?

—Does the sound they create have a good effect on you?

—What can you learn about the technical aspects of playing by watching and/or listening to them?

—What can you learn from their improvisations?

—Do they present themselves well and with dignity? Do they have a pleasant demeanor?

The idea here is to have you discover for yourself where you can be most effective within the field of music by learning from or imitating the ways of others who have already found their place. Considering the vast scope of music that a contempoary bassist must be familiar with, it is important to define one's own place early on in one's development.

Of course these considerations can change in time as one learns and expands, and indeed it is good to remain flexible and flow with the changes that occur in music and your own life. Surviving as a musician is tough, and much can be learned by observing those who have survived and continue to survive artistically, financially, physically, mentally, and spiritually.

Basically the purpose of playing music is to bring some joy, fun, enlightenment, and pleasure to people. Considering the present condition of humanity, there could be no finer purpose than this.

Now we will proceed to outline a method of practicing designed to give the most benefit for the time you invest.

1. **Decide on a specific time span to be used** One hour of concentrated work is far superior to several hours of scattered attention.

2. **Decide on a specific problem** Look at your list of weak points. How can you improve them? Take one at a time and work on it.

3. **Don't take on more than you can handle within the chosen time span** Set a goal—one page or one exercise, for example—and meet it. If you meet your goal before the time is up, set another goal. Rest before beginning again.

4. **Don't waste time practicing your strong points** Save this for when you're performing. Remember, practicing is to add to your strong points by overcoming weak ones.

5. **If something comes up which is confusing to you, don't pass over it** Stop and go back to the point where it wasn't confusing and find out where the confusion arose and clear it up before continuing. This is very important.

6. **Have fun!** Practicing need not be drudgery. Keep it light, challenge yourself, make a game out of it and win!

Tuning the Bass

The bass is tuned in fourths from the lowest note upwards.

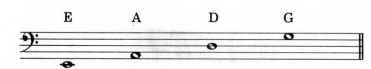

The best way to tune is with harmonics. These can be found on the twelfth, seventh, and fifth frets. Harmonics are sounded by placing the finger on the note (right over the fret) without pressing it down, and bowing, plucking, or picking that note.

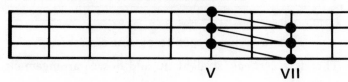

The lines show the unison relationships between harmonics on adjacent strings.

The Range of the Bass

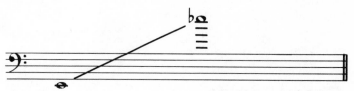

The range of the bass is two octaves and a major seventh. Acoustic basses go higher, as do some custom made electric basses. The actual pitch of the notes sound one octave lower than they are written. The most frequently used range is:

The available notes within the written range are as follows:

Natural notes (No sharps or flats)

Name:	E	F	G	A	B	C	D	E	F	G	A	B	C	D	E	F	G	A	B	C	D
Fret:	0	1	3	0	2	3	0	2	3	0	2	4	5	7	9	10	12	14	16	17	19

Sharp notes

F#	G#	A#	C#	D#	F#	G#	A#	C#	D#	F#	G#	A#	C#	D#
2	4	1	4	1	4	1	3	6	8	11	13	15	18	20

Flat notes

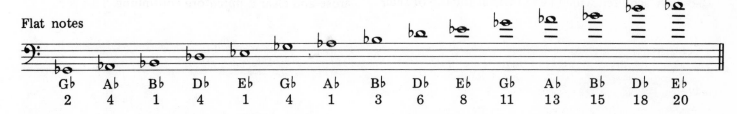

Gb	Ab	Bb	Db	Eb	Gb	Ab	Bb	Db	Eb	Gb	Ab	Bb	Db	Eb
2	4	1	4	1	4	1	3	6	8	11	13	15	18	20

Study Assignment—Note Reading

Since a professional bassist is expected to be able to read any note within the written range of the bass, the first study assignment is to learn and commit to memory all of the natural, sharp, and flat notes and play them on the instrument. In addition to looking at the charts, another good way to become familiar with the notes is to write them out yourself on some music manuscript.

This is one of the most important assignments in this book. Complete it *thoroughly* before proceeding. Use the following as a check list to help your concentration:

—Learn the names of the notes.
—Learn their position on the music staff.
—Learn their position on the bass.

Scales

Chord Scales

A common problem for many student bassists is an uncertainty as to the correct notes to play through the chords found in jazz and contemporary music.

In order to create a musically correct and appropriate bass line through a given chord, it is necessary to know the scale from which the chord is made. Basically, scales exist to allow the composer or player a choice of notes related to a given chord. These serve to create melodies or bass lines with some kind of logical sequence that can express a particular emotion or idea.

Chord scales represent to the improvising musician what colors represent to a painter. Before a painter can create an exciting or meaningful image he must acquire skill in using the materials of his craft. He must have a thorough knowledge of colors and how to combine them in a composition. It is similar for a musician who improvises—the chord scales are his colors. Some are "bright"; some are "dark." (There is an explanation of this in the section on modes.)

A knowledge of the chord scales and how they function is a good starting point to the end of improvising bass parts and solos in a free flowing style, and it can be applied equally well in a number of styles. When playing through the scales, begin to note the differences in each one and how they feel to you. Find areas in your own sphere of musical activity where you could apply them. Before you begin, read the definition of chord scales and be clear on them. If you wish to know more about the theoretical construction of scales, refer to the chapter on intervals.

Chord Scales: Definitions

Chord: A combination of three or more notes or tones, sounded together at the same time.

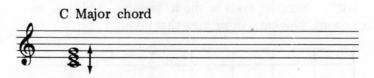

This is a *vertical* (straight up and down) arrangement of notes.

Scale: A series of notes or tones arranged in a sequence of rising or falling pitches within one octave.

This is a *horizontal* or *linear* arrangement of notes.

It follows that a chord scale is a series of notes arranged in horizontal or linear form that contains within it all the notes of a given chord.

Chord-Scale Chart

Symbols: △ =Major, – =Minor, + =Augmented, o =Diminished, ø = Half Diminished

C-7(♭5) can also use Half Diminished (ø) scale.
For example:

C-7(♭5) (Half Diminished)

There are many other possible scales. The ones given above represent the most commonly used ones. Some of the chords given may be unfamiliar to the student, so an explanation of certain chords—Lydian Major Seventh, Lydian Dominant Seventh, Dominant Seventh, Diminished chords—and their practical functions—is offered at a further point in this book.

Since it is beyond the scope of this book to cover the subject of basic harmony and jazz harmony, it would help the student who has not covered this subject to have some instruction either through a teacher or with a textbook. An excellent book on the subject is *Improvising Jazz* by Jerry Coker.

Practice Method for Chord Scales

The following section deals with a way to gain fluency of technique and familiarity with each of the scales on the chord-scale chart.

They can be played on both acoustic and electric bass, with a bow, fingers, or pick. This is a large assignment. Don't attempt to do it in a hurry. Take one step at a time until you feel completely comfortable with the scale in question. Use a metronome! This will greatly develop your ability to maintain an even tempo and accuracy in placement of notes. Work up to the speed you want to achieve:

1. Set it at slow tempo
2. Set it at medium tempo
3. Set it at fast tempo

Take your time, do it right, and you'll have remarkable gains in ability!

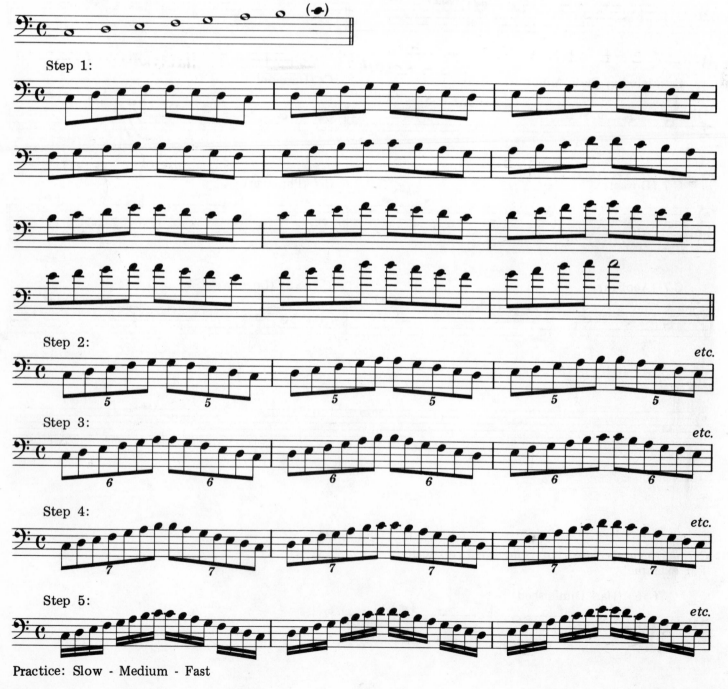

Practice: Slow - Medium - Fast

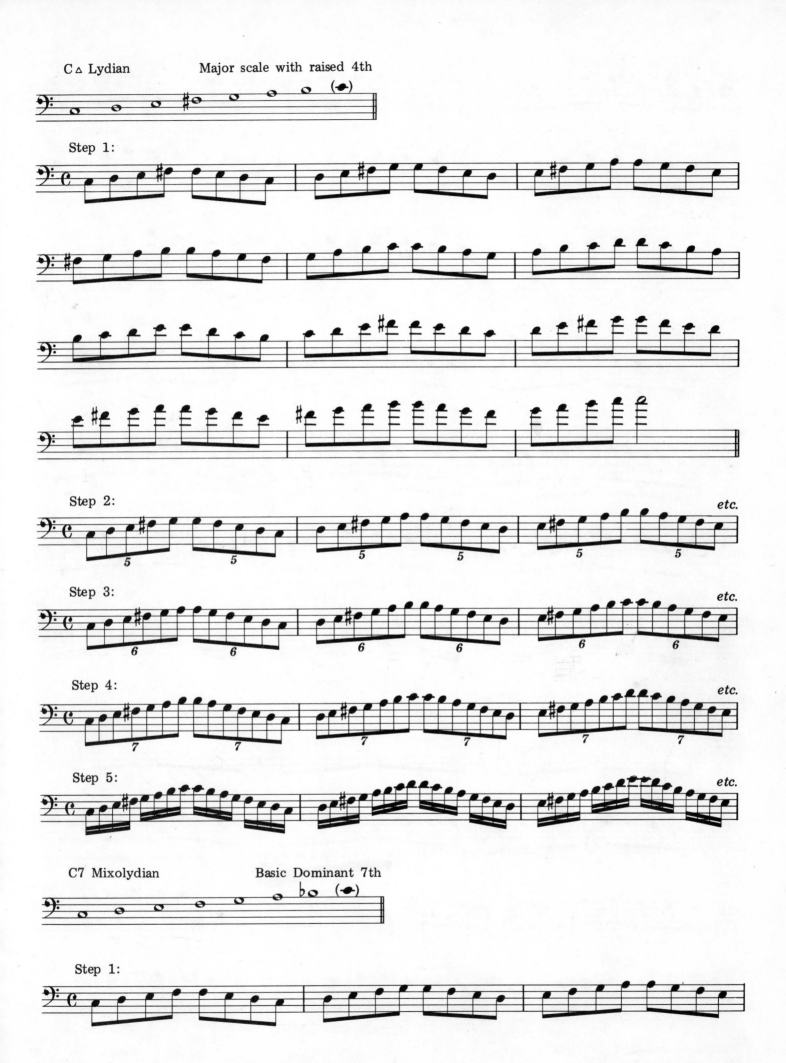

C△ Lydian   Major scale with raised 4th

Step 1:

Step 2:   etc.

Step 3:   etc.

Step 4:   etc.

Step 5:   etc.

C7 Mixolydian   Basic Dominant 7th

Step 1:

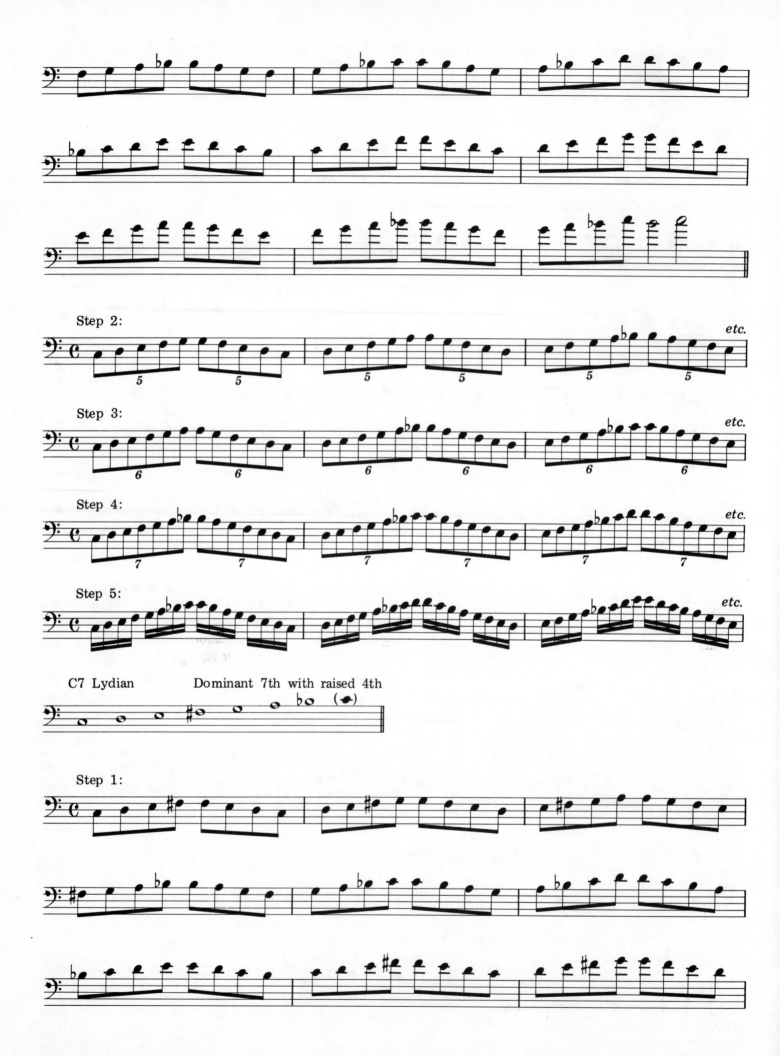

Step 2:

Step 3:

Step 4:

Step 5:

C7 Lydian   Dominant 7th with raised 4th

Step 1:

Step 2:

Step 3:

Step 4:

Step 5:

Functions of Lydian Major 7th and Lydian Dominant 7th Chords

In the chord-scale chart there are two chords which are often misunderstood. Basically, the Lydian Major 7th chord scale is the familiar major scale except that the fourth note of the scale is raised by one half-step.

The Lydian Dominant 7th chord scale is the familiar Dominant Mixolydian scale, except that the fourth note is also raised one half-step. The most common use of these two chords is as *substitute chords** to aid in producing smooth *voice leading*—the manner in which the inner parts of a chord move to another chord—and smooth bass motion.

Key of C Major

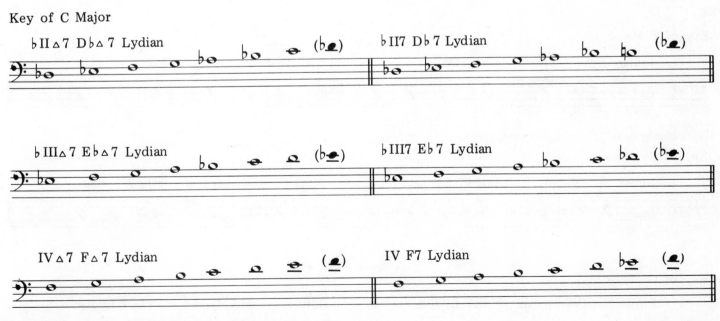

Substitute chord: a chord used in place of the usual chord for added interest and harmonic taste.

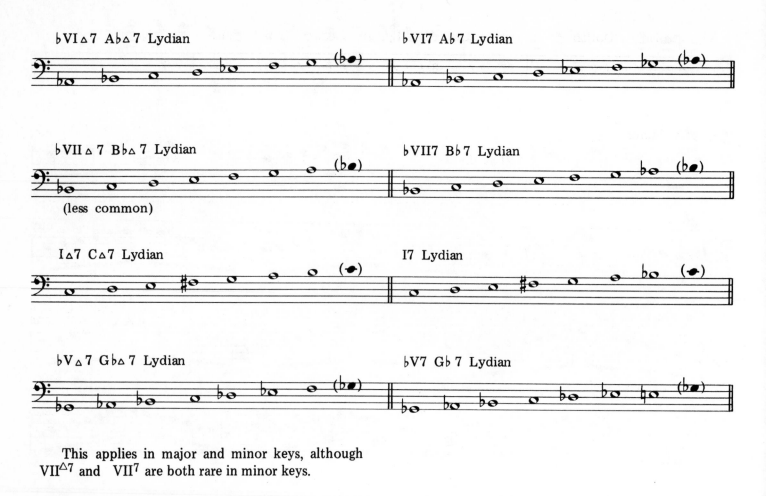

This applies in major and minor keys, although
VII$^{\triangle 7}$ and   VII^7 are both rare in minor keys.

Chord Progressions Using
Lydian Major 7th and
Lydian Dominant 7th Chords

Key of C Major

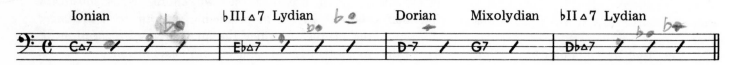

Key of F Major

Key of Bb Major

Key of G Major

18

Study Assignment—Lydian Chords

1. Write out on some music paper the Lydian Major 7th and Lydian Dominant 7th chord-scales and their corresponding chord symbols in the places they can occur. Do this for each of the following keys:

Db major
F minor
D major
Gb minor
Eb major
G minor

2. Write out several chord progressions that incorporate Lydian chords.

3. Play the Lydian scales in the six different keys from exercise 1.

4. Figure out the correct modal scales for the chord progressions you wrote out in exercise 2.

Altered Dominant 7th Chords

On C^7 Mixolydian (basic dominant 7th scale) the intervals *above* the octave are:

On C^7 Altered the intervals *above* the octave are:

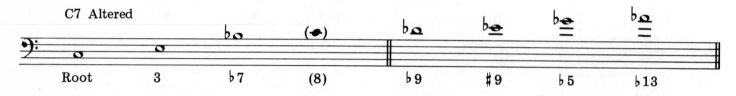

Employ the usual practice method for these Altered Dominant 7th chords.

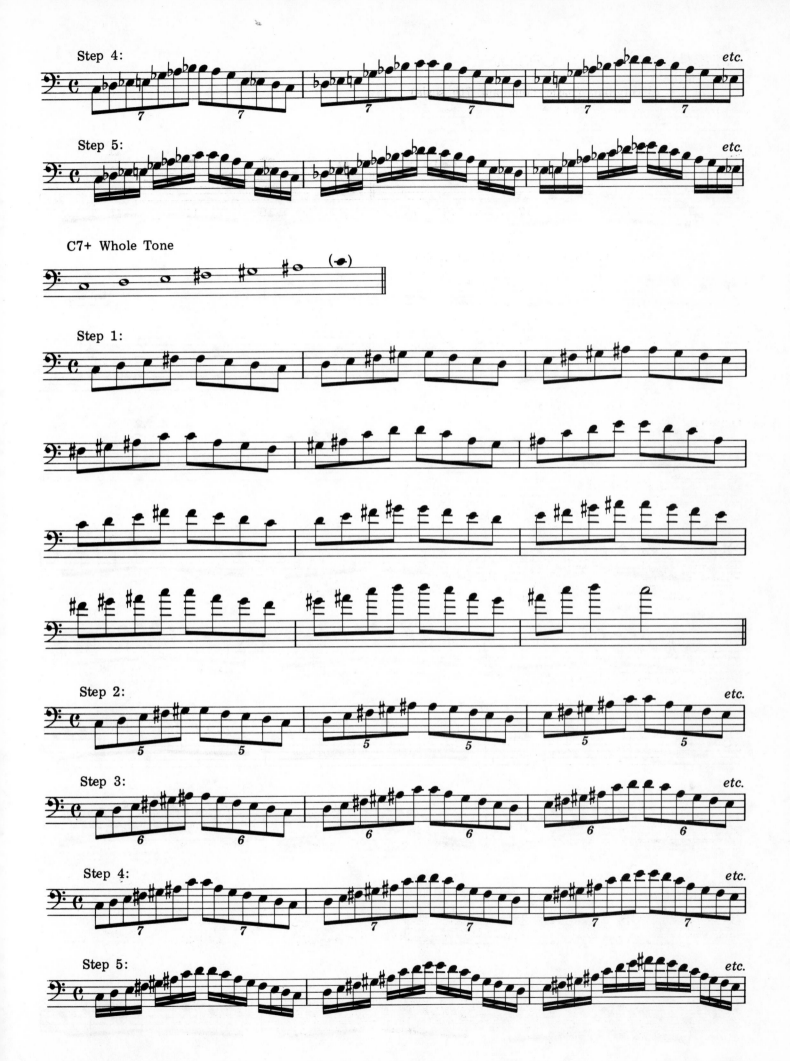

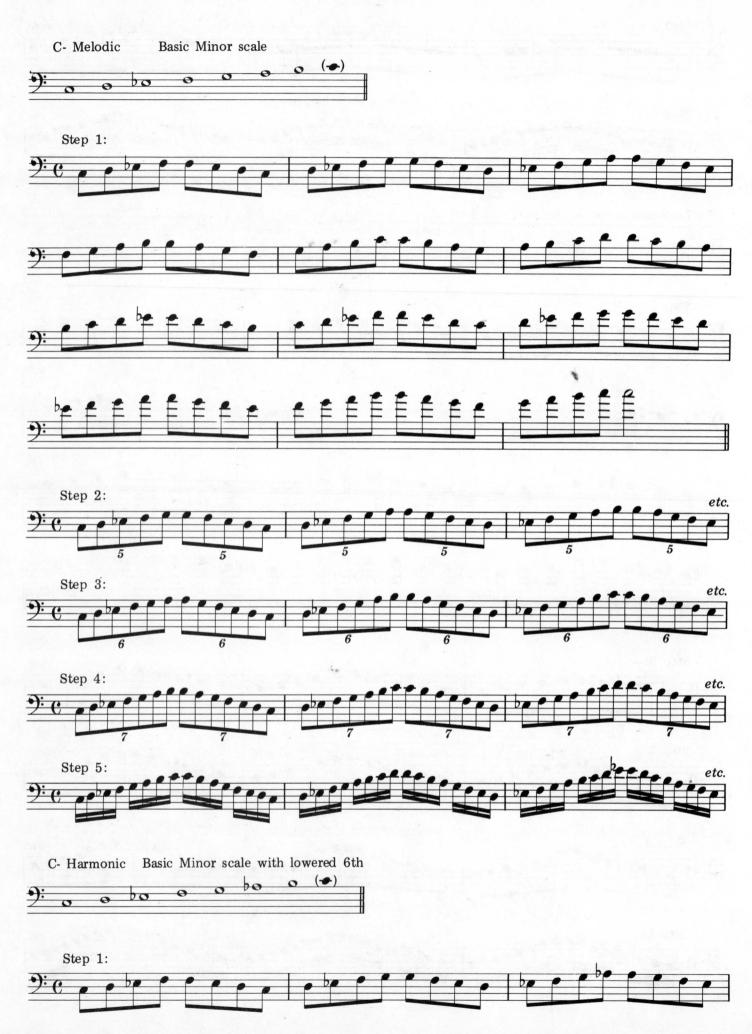

C- Melodic   Basic Minor scale

Step 1:

Step 2:   *etc.*

Step 3:   *etc.*

Step 4:   *etc.*

Step 5:   *etc.*

C- Harmonic   Basic Minor scale with lowered 6th

Step 1:

22

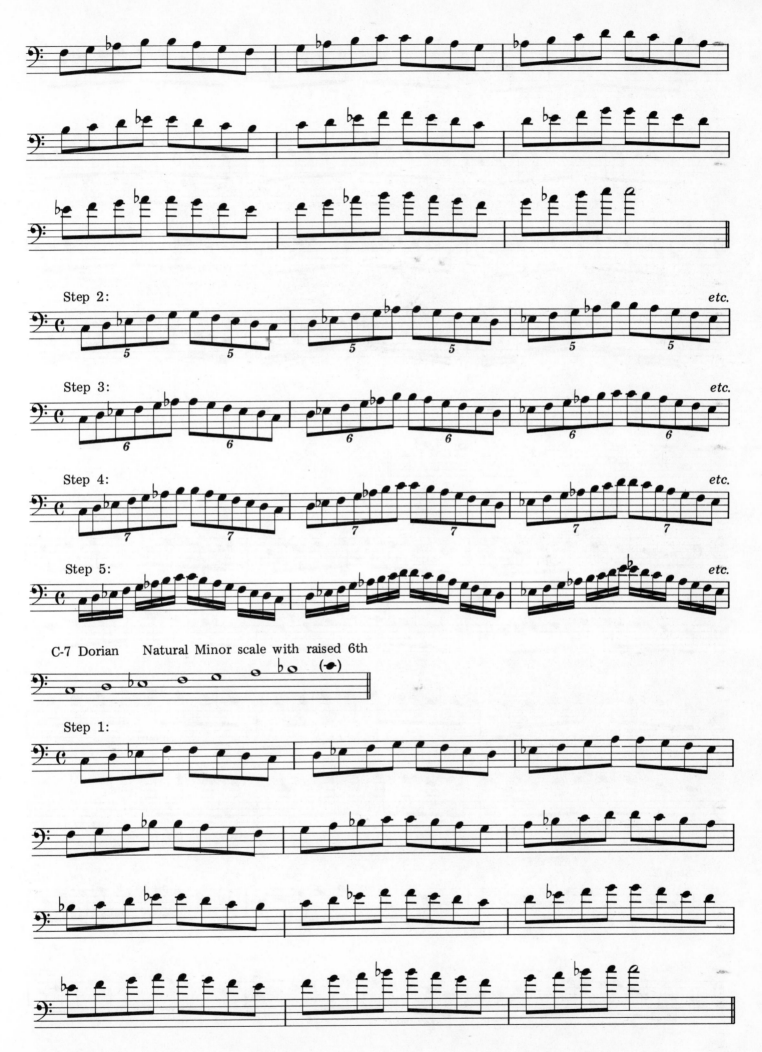

Step 2:

Step 3:

Step 4:

Step 5:

C-7 Dorian   Natural Minor scale with raised 6th

Step 1:

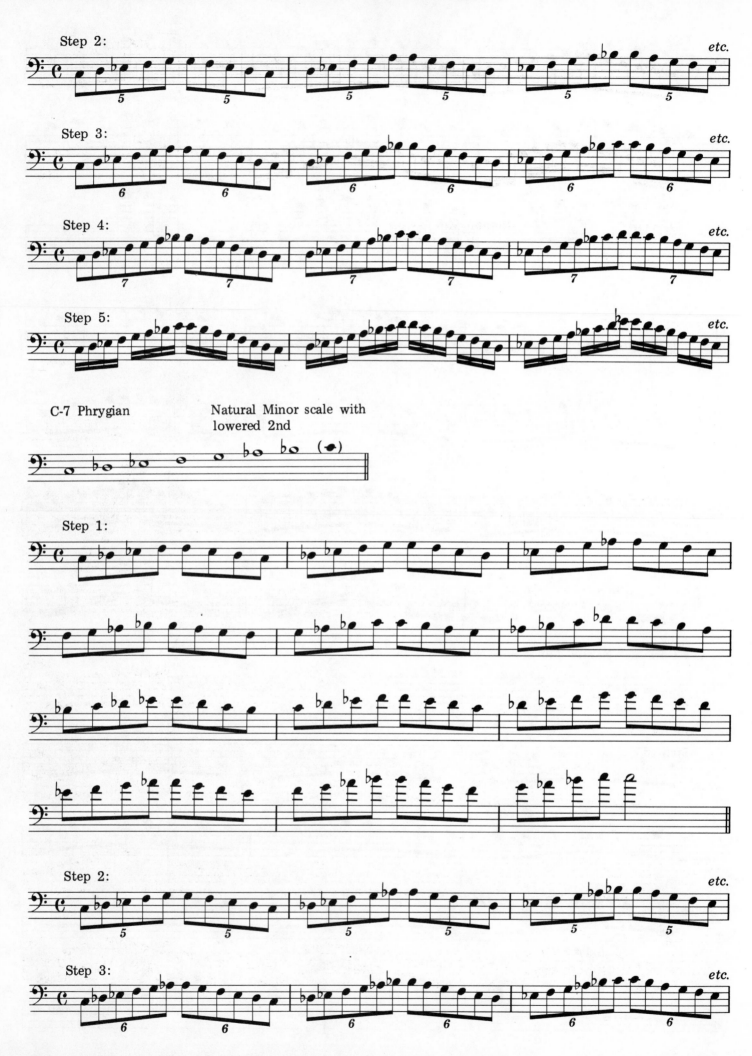

Step 2: *etc.*

Step 3: *etc.*

Step 4: *etc.*

Step 5: *etc.*

C-7 Phrygian   Natural Minor scale with
lowered 2nd

Step 1:

Step 2: *etc.*

Step 3: *etc.*

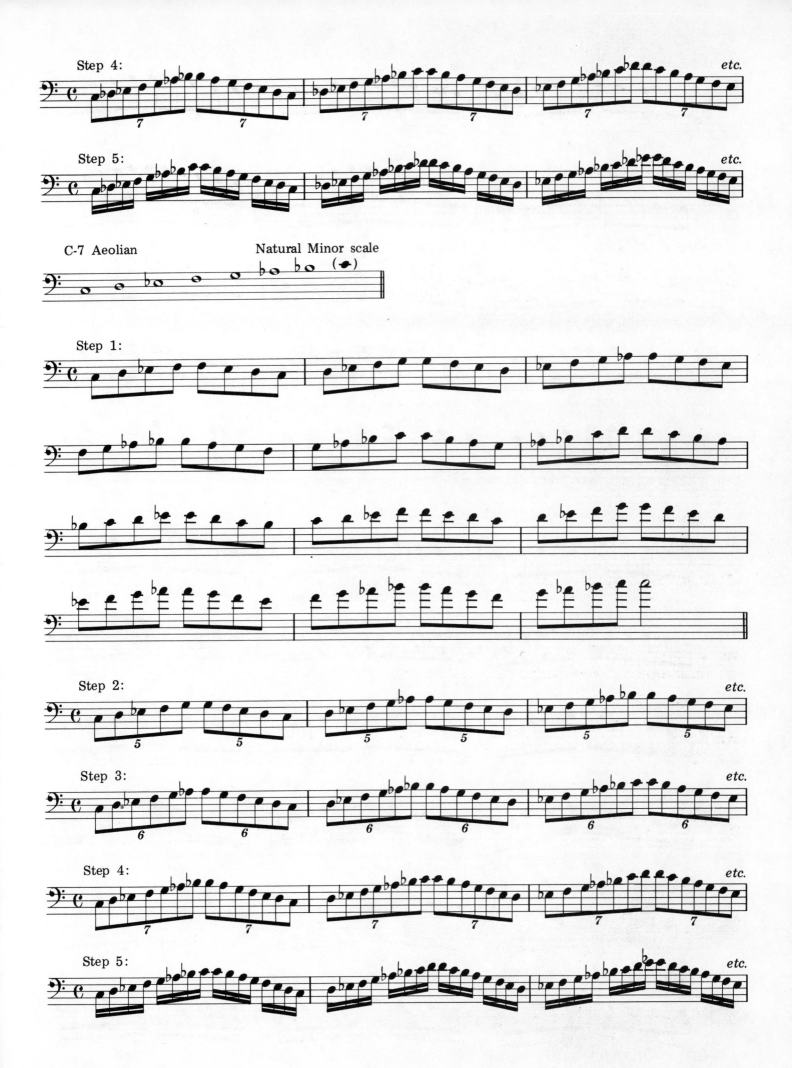

Natural Minor scale with
lowered 2nd, and 5th

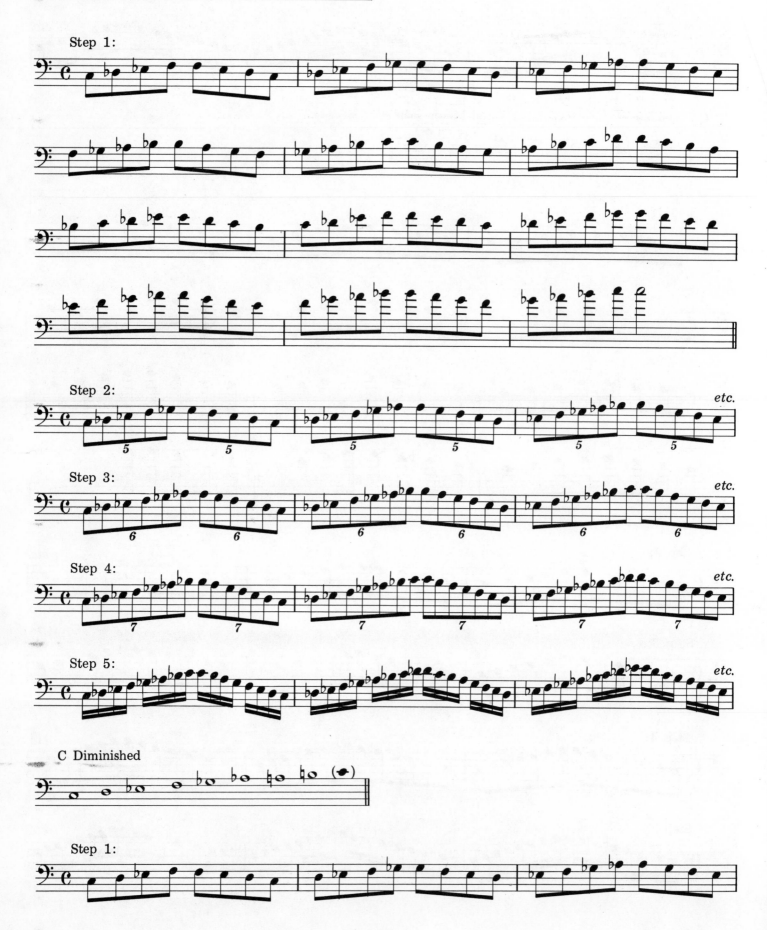

Step 1:

Step 2:

Step 3:

Step 4:

Step 5:

C Diminished

Step 1:

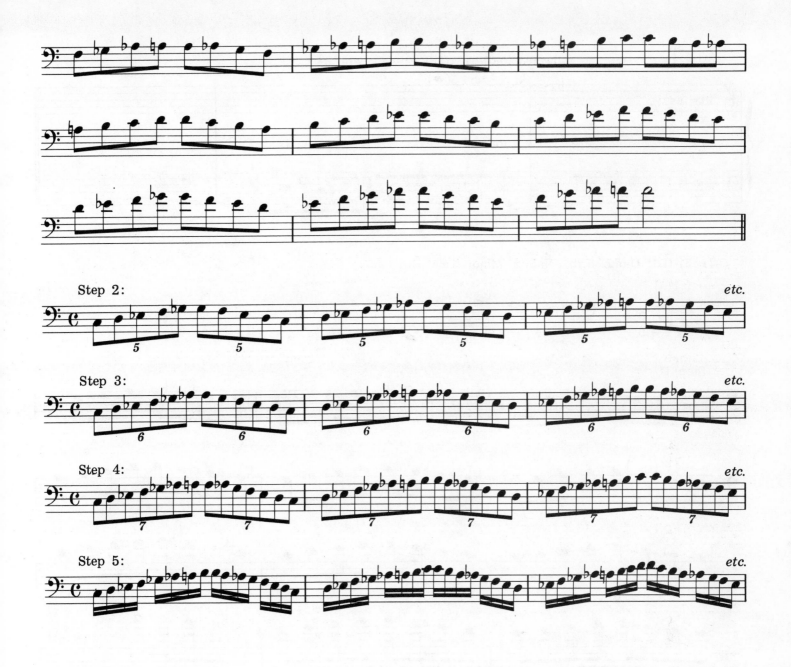

Diminished Scales

Diminished scales can work well with a number of chords *other* than Diminished chords.

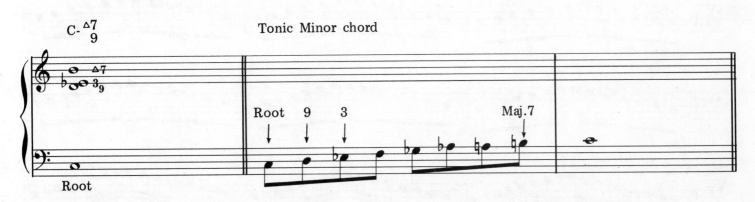

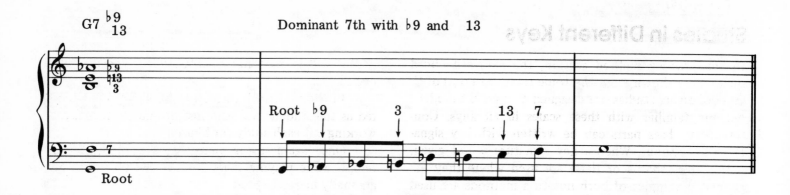

C-7(♭5) Half Diminished   Natural Minor scale with
                          lowered 5th

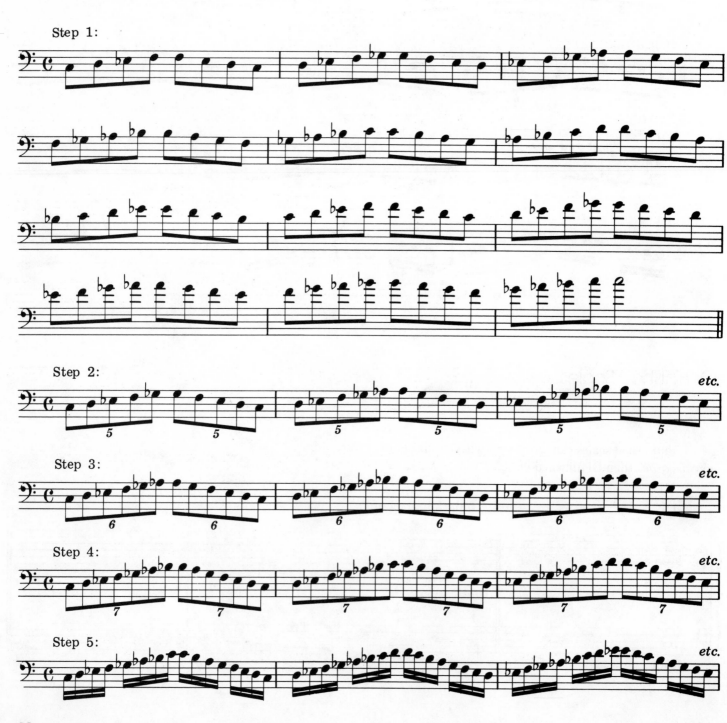

Chord Scales:
Studies in Different Keys

In the practice method section, the fourteen chord scales were shown from the tonic (starting note) of C. The following studies are designed to have the student become familiar with these scales in all keys. Contemporary bass parts can be written with key signatures or without. When a key signature is not given, *accidentals* (sharps or flats) are used where they are needed. Examples of both notation methods are used as this will greatly increase the student's reading skill in all keys.

In addition, fingering has deliberately been omitted as the student will gain insight and proficiency by working out each study for himself.

Once again, use a metronome to keep a steady tempo while playing these studies. Start *slowly*, then gradually increase speed.

E△ Ionian (Basic Major)

F△

G♭△

G△

A♭△

A△

B♭△

B△

C△

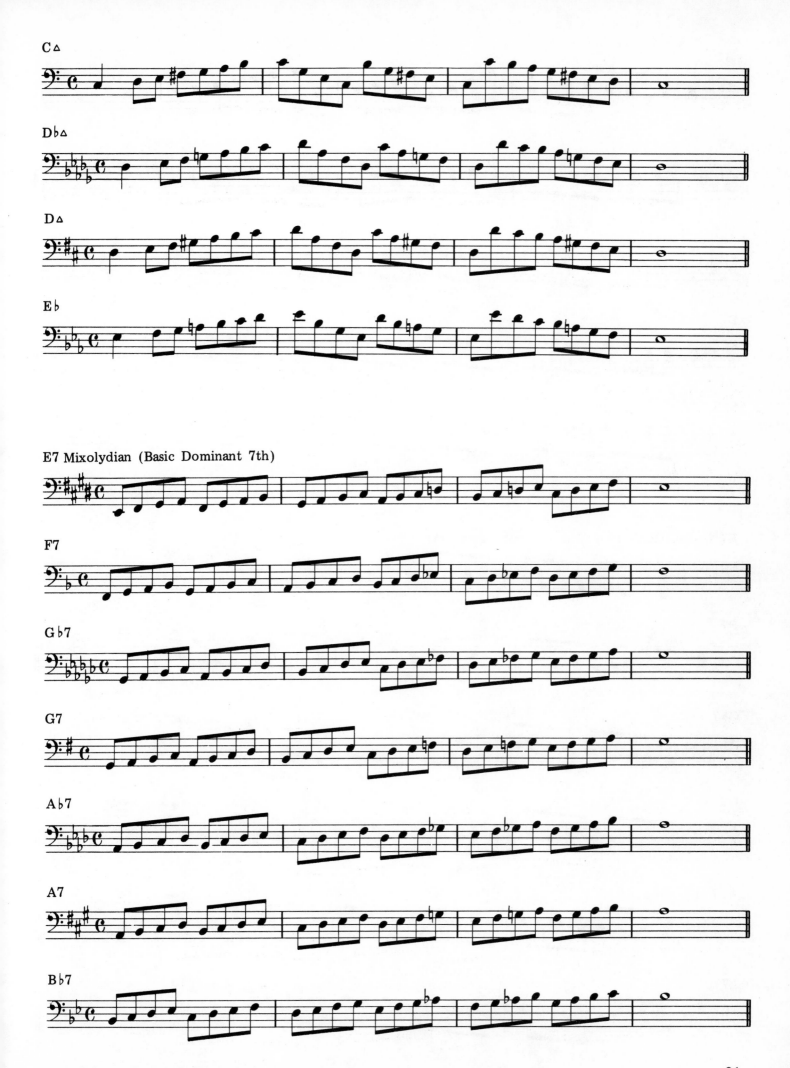

E- Harmonic (Basic Minor with lowered 6th)

E-7 Dorian (Minor 7th with natural 6th)

F-7

G♭-7 (variation)

G-7

A♭-7

A-7 (variation)

B♭-7

B-7

C-7 (variation)

D♭-7 (variation)

D-7

Eb-7 (variation)

E-7 Phrygian (Minor 7th with lowered 2nd)

F-7

Gb-7

G-7 (variation)

Ab-7

A-7 (variation)

Bb-7

B-7

C-7 (variation)

Db-7

D-7

Eb-7 (variation)

E-7 Aeolian (Minor 7th with lowered 6th)

F-7

Gb-7

G-7 (variation)

Ab-7

A-7

Bb-7 (variation)

B-7

Pentatonic Scales

The word pentatonic is derived from *penta*, meaning five, and *tonic*, referring to tones. Thus, a pentatonic scale is a five-note scale.

The use of pentatonic scales is quite common in all forms of contemporary music, and especially so in improvisation, for example, John Coltrane's solo on "Giant Steps" from the album *Giant Steps*.

Pentatonic scales can be used in both bass lines and solo material. Although they are diatonic, there is an inherent tonal ambiguity due to their "incompleteness" as compared to a seven-note chord-scale.

There are many possible pentatonic scales. Some of the most common ones are: *diatonic*, *pelog*, *hirajoshi*, and *kumoi*. These last three are derived from Japanese music, much of which is based on the notes of these scales.

Each scales has its own inversions.

Play each scale and its inversions.

Pentatonic Scales:
Studies in Different Keys

49

A (variation)

50

Pentatonic Scales within Chord Scales

These pentatonics within the chord scales are some of the more practical ones for general use. Play each chord scale, then play the pentatonics within it.

C△ Ionian

Diatonic   Diatonic

C△ Lydian

Diatonic   Diatonic

C7 Mixolydian

Diatonic   Diatonic (Key of B♭, 1st inversion)

C7 Lydian

Diatonic   Kumoi

C7 Altered

Diatonic (Key of G♭, 3rd inversion)   Kumoi

C- Melodic

Kumoi   Diatonic (Key of F, 4th inversion)

C- Harmonic

Hirajoshi

C-7 Dorian

Diatonic (Key of E♭, 4th inversion)   Kumoi

C-7 Phrygian

Diatonic (Key of E♭, 4th inversion)   Pelog

C-7 Aeolian

Diatonic
(Key of E♭, 4th inversion)

Hirajoshi

C-7 Locrian

Kumoi

C-7(♭5) Half Diminished

Kumoi

One pentatonic scale, or its inversions, can work
through many different chord scales:

Diatonic   C△ Ionian   C△ Lydian

C7 Mixolydian   C7 Lydian   F△ Lydian

G7 Mixolydian   G-7 Dorian   D-7 Dorian

D-7 Aeolian   A-7 Aeolian   A-7 Dorian

G♭7 Altered   E-7 Phrygian   B♭△ Lydian

A-7 Phrygian   D7 Mixolydian   G- Melodic

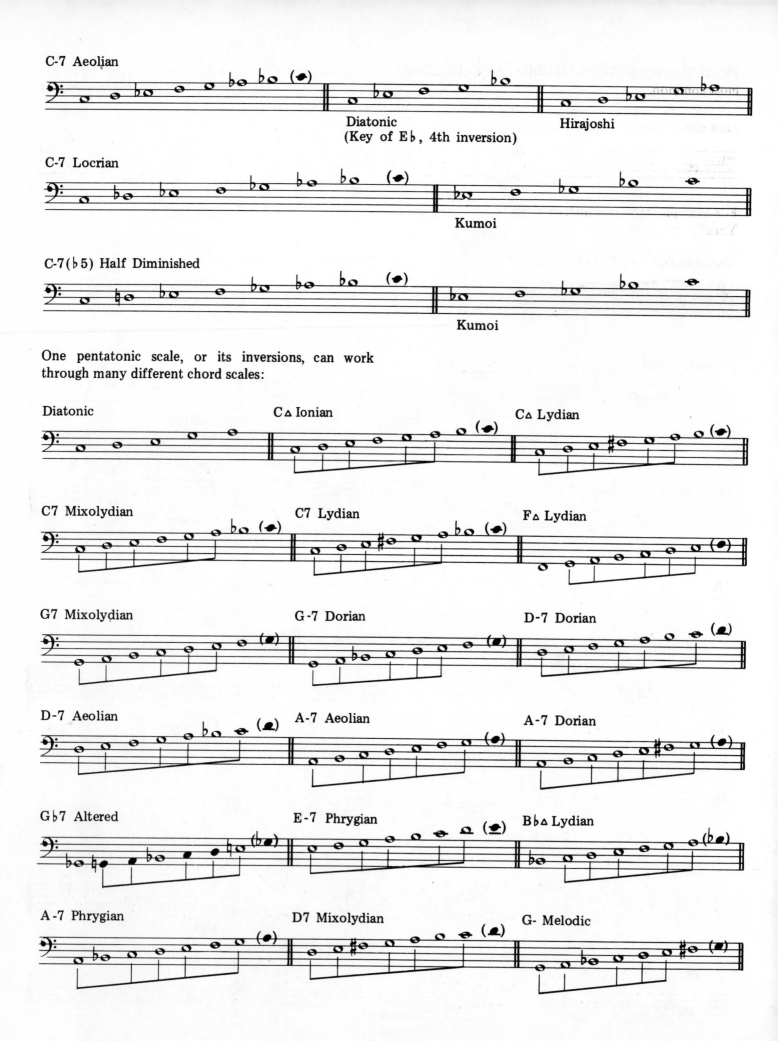

Of all of these scales, the diatonic pentatonic is the most common.

Note that in a C major scale, the two notes which are omitted are B and F, thus avoiding the ambiguous sound of the tritone.

Diatonic

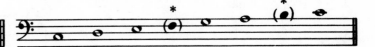

For example, take this melody from "Autumn in New York":

Diatonic (Key of F, 3rd inversion)

Examples Using Pentatonic Scales

In the following examples, we will look at some ways to use the diatonic pentatonic scale in an actual playing situation.

Rock
A-

Diatonic (4th inversion)

Rock
C

Diatonic (Root position)

An example using it as a solo or a melodic line is:

A-

Here is the same solo/melodic line using different chords:

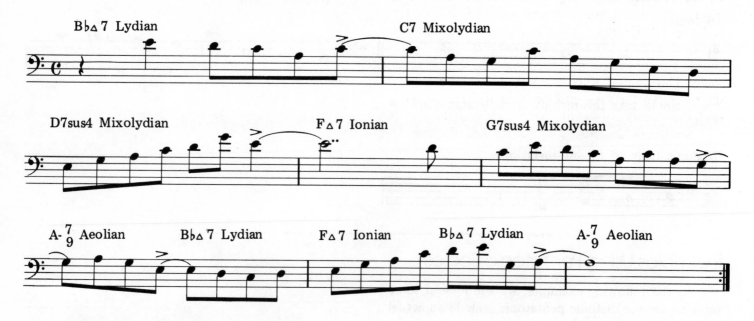

The following is an example of combining two pentatonic scales on the same chord:

Diatonic

Diatonic
(Key of B♭, 1st inversion)

Study Assignment—Pentatonics

1. Select a chord scale, find the pentatonic(s) that work with it, and make up a rock bass line.

2. Select a chord scale, find the pentatonic(s) that work with it, and make up a solo or melodic line. Then see how many different chords you can use with the solo or melodic line.

3. How many chord scales can you find for the following pentatonics?

Modal Scales

Of the fourteen chord scales listed in the chord-scale chart, seven stand apart because of their whole-step/half-step relationship. These are called *modes*. A piece of music can be based around one tone with all the chords (harmonies) gravitating towards this tone, or *tonic*. This central tone establishes the modality of the piece. To further a study of modes, refer to *Twentieth Century Harmony*, by Vincent Persichetti.

Modal music is quite common in jazz. A good example is the tune "So What" recorded by Miles Davis on the album *Kind of Blue*.

The seven modal scales are as follows (arrows indicate the characteristic tone of each mode):

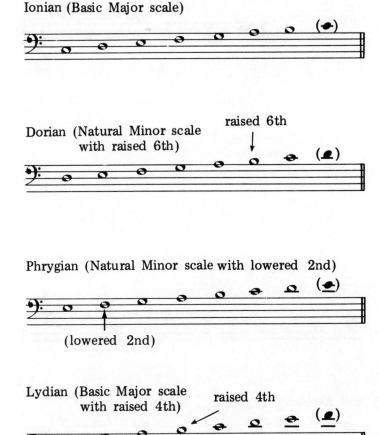

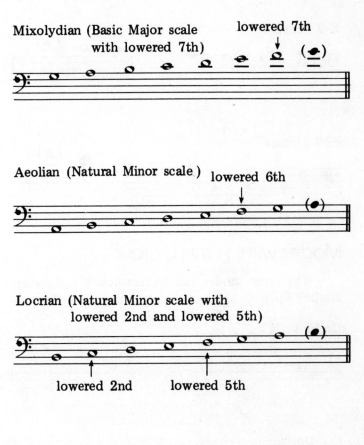

The chord symbols which correspond to each mode are:

C△7 Ionian (Basic Major)

G7 Mixolydian

D-7 Dorian

A-7 Aeolian

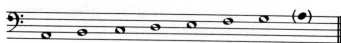

E-7 Phrygian

B-7(♭5) Locrian

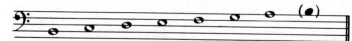

F△7 Lydian

Modes within One Octave

The seven modes can be transposed to the same starting point to assist in distinguishing the difference.

C△ Ionian

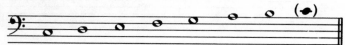

C7 Mixolydian

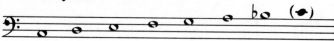

C-7 Dorian

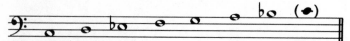

C-7 Aeolian

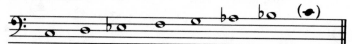

C-7 Phrygian

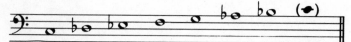

C-7 Locrian

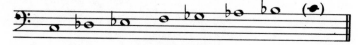

C△7 Lydian

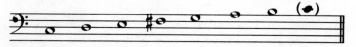

The "darkest" modes have the most number of flats. The "brightest" modes have the least number of flats.

Darkest	Dark	Bright	Brightest
Locrian	Phrygian	Dorian	Ionian
	Aeolian	Mixolydian	Lydian

Establishing Modes

A mode can be established by using chords that gravitate around a central point and *cadence* (definition: arrive at a point of rest) to this central point. For example:

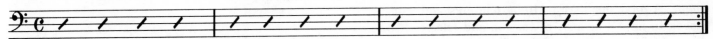

Thus, the mode of this chord sequence would be Aeolian.

One mode can be used for an entire section:

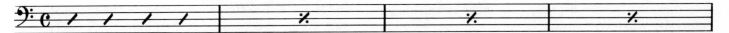

In the second example, the bassist, the chordal instruments, and the soloist would all improvise parts based on the Dorian scale.

Another way to establish modality is to have the characteristic tone of the central mode emphasized in the melody:

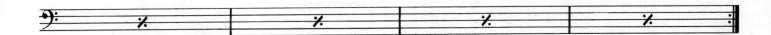

However, the bassist, in accompanying a melody instrument playing the above line, would probably do best to emphasize the root of the chord so that the raised 4th does not obscure the tonal center.

The application of modes to walking bass lines and soloing will be covered in a later chapter.

Study Assignment—Modes

1. Write out on some music paper the notes and corresponding chord symbols of the seven modes in the following key centers:

Db
E
G
Bb

2. Name the characteristic tone of:
a.   the Lydian mode
b.   the Dorian mode
c.   the Phrygian mode
d.   the Mixolydian mode
e.   the Aeolian mode
f.   the Locrian mode

3. In key center of Eb Major which mode would be
a.   darkest?
b.   brightest?

4. Write out a chord progression—about four bars—that gravitates to the key center of E-7 Dorian.

Scale Analysis and Intervals

The purpose of this chapter is to have the student get familiar with the various components of each scale and learn to apply them when improvising bass parts and solos.

Melodic lines and bass lines are comprised of a sequence of notes based on the chord scale of the moment. A good line, in order to have interest and impact, needs to have a balance of tension and release. If one were to play just up and down the basic chord scale, it would get pretty monotonous.

The idea here is to examine each scale and see which *intervals* (definition: the space between each pair of notes) are *consonant* (definition: in harmonic agreement with each other) and *dissonant* (definition: not in harmonic agreement with each other). A good line then, is a balance between consonant and dissonant intervals: Whatever tension is caused by dissonance is released by consonance.

C△ (Ionian)

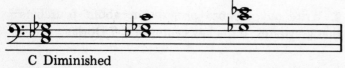

Scale Analysis

Each scale contains within it the material used for the melody, harmony, and bass part. The best way to find out what is available in a scale is to examine the components. For example:

The first step is to find the *triads* within a scale. A triad is a three-note chord—it can be major, minor, augmented, or diminished—in any one of its three inversions. For example:

First Position   Second Position   Third position

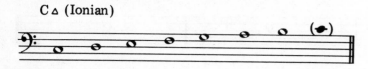

C Major

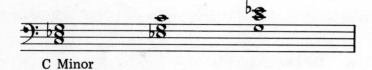

C Minor

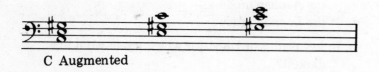

C Augmented

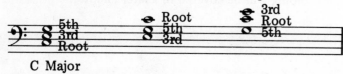

C Diminished

The triads of a C major scale,

C△ Ionian (Basic Major scale)

are as follows:

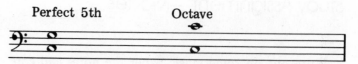

C△   D-   E-   F△   G△   A-   B°

Types of Intervals

The second step is to categorize the intervals within the scale. The following is a list of the types of intervals, arranged according to their harmonic *quality*.

Consonant Intervals	Dissonant Intervals
Octave	Minor 2nd
Perfect 5th	Major 7th
Major 3rd	Major 2nd
Minor 3rd	Minor 7th
Major 6th	Tritone (augmented 4th or diminished 5th)
Perfect 4th (can also be dissonant)	Perfect 4th

In this list, the qualities of the intervals are:

octave, perfect 5th — *open consonance*

major and minor 3rd and 6th — *soft consonance*

minor 2nd, major 7th — *sharp dissonance*

major 2nd, minor 7th — *mild dissonance*

perfect 4th — *consonance* or *dissonance*

tritone — *ambiguous* (can be *neutral* or *restless*)

The most consonant intervals are the perfect 5th and the octave.

Perfect 5th   Octave

The most dissonant intervals are the minor 2nd and the major 7th.

Minor 2nd   Major 7th

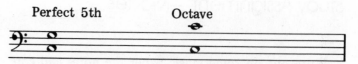

Intervals and Their Inversions

The reversal of the tones in an interval by raising the lower tone one octave will give you the inversion of that interval. For example:

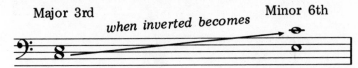

Below is a chart of all the intervals related to C and their inversions.

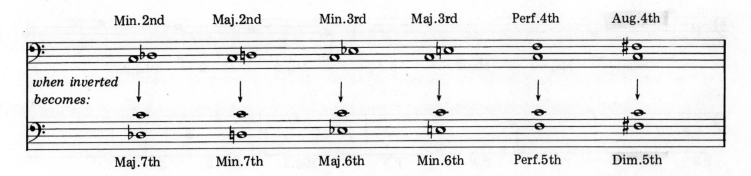

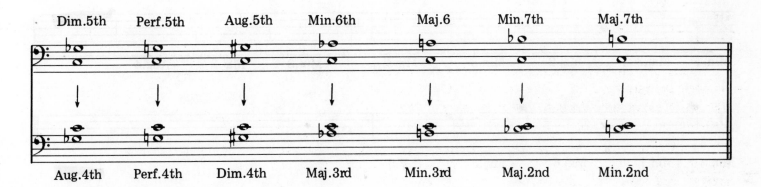

The intervals in a C major scale,

C △ (Ionian)

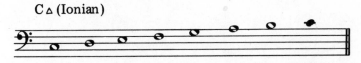

are:

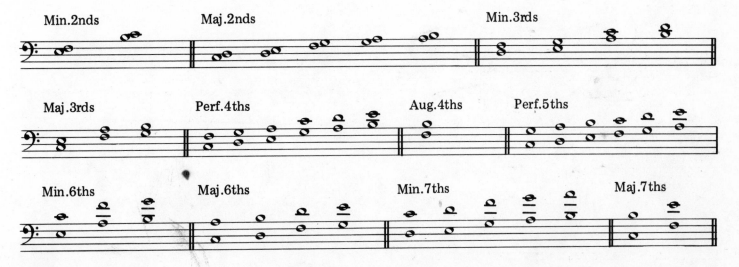

The example below uses various intervals and their inversions to make a bass line "walk." (Refer also to the chapter, *Making a Walking Bass Line*.) Play through this bass line slowly, and name each interval as you sound it on the instrument.

C Major

C△7

Octave Maj.6 Maj.2 p.4 Maj.2 Min.2 Maj.2

P.5 Maj.7 P.5 P.4 P.5 Maj.2 Min.2 .Min.6

Min.3 Maj.3 Maj.2 Min.3 Min.2 Min.3 Maj.2 Aug.4

Min.2 Min.7 Maj.6 Maj.3 P.5

Below is an example of a melodic solo line using the available intervals in a scale. Once again, play through this solo *slowly* and name each interval as you sound it on the instrument.

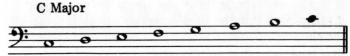

C Major

Obviously, in an actual playing situation one would not be able to sit down and figure out the various intervals of all the chords and scales in a piece of music. Improvisation is an art, and the art of it is in the quality of communication. There are many aspects of improvisation which are difficult to verbalize, as it is a highly aesthetic art form and each individual artist has his or her own unique way of expressing musical feelings and ideas.

Analyzing chord scales and intervals is a somewhat intellectual, dry kind of process and is not an end in itself. Music of quality in any idiom is a balance of all the qualities of the individual artist—if it were all intellectual it would tend to alienate an audience. However, this is a subjective viewpiont; what is meaningful music to one person may leave another totally unaffected. The purpose of the preceding material is to have you assimilate into your musical "computer" the information on intervals with the end of being able to draw on this information freely. Remember the comparison to the way a painter draws on his knowledge of colors and the various ways they can be mixed to produce an effect.

Study Assignment—Intervals

1. Work out on paper the various intervals contained in each of the fourteen chord scales.

2. Select some chord scales at random and make:
a. short examples of walking bass lines using various intervals from the chosen chord scale.
b. melodic bass solo from a selected chord scale.

Play through your examples.

3. Take some written melodies and figure out the interval from each note to the next.

About Bass Lines

Reading Bass Parts

The overall skill of being able to read contemporary bass parts can be subdivided into three components. One should be able to recognize and play immediately (sightread) the notes in the bass clef, the rhythms in which these notes are set, and the chord symbols and scales related to them.

Reading music is actually the ability to duplicate or interpret the composer's or arranger's ideas as closely as possible and reproduce them clearly on the instrument. We have already covered the notes in the bass clef, and the chord symbols and related scales, therefore the next component to examine is that of reading rhythms. Before doing this, the rudiments of music are offered. The student is urged to learn these rudiments thoroughly as any misunderstandings can cause confusion and uncertainty further on.

Notation Symbols

Rhythmic Values

Notes

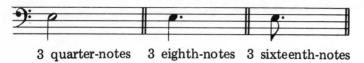

| Rests | Whole | Half | Quarter | Eighth | Sixteenth |

A dot after a note or rest increases its value by one-half.

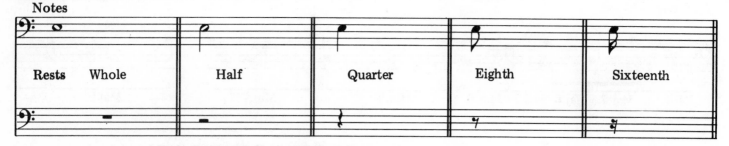

3 quarter-notes   3 eighth-notes   3 sixteenth-notes

Attack Marks

long   short   accent   slide up   slide off

Dynamic Markings

p	*mp*	*mf*	*f*	*ff*
piano	mezzo piano	mezzo forte	forte	fortissimo
soft	medium soft	medium loud	loud	very loud

Time Signatures

The terms *time signature* and *meter* refer to the pattern of musical pulsations, or *beats*.

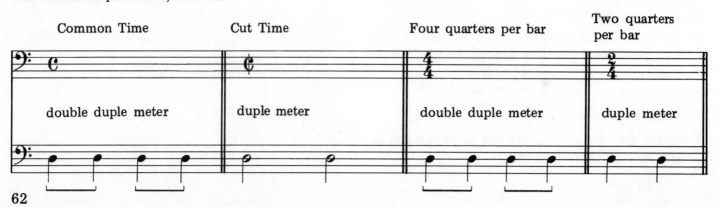

| Common Time | Cut Time | Four quarters per bar | Two quarters per bar |
| double duple meter | duple meter | double duple meter | duple meter |

62

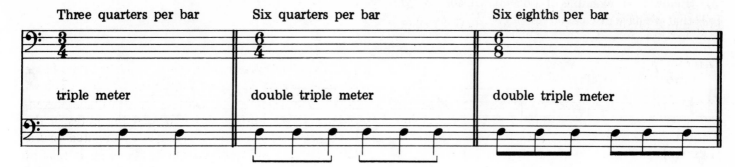

Three quarters per bar	Six quarters per bar	Six eighths per bar
triple meter	double triple meter	double triple meter

Clefs

Treble, or G, clef *(indicates G)*

Bass, or F, clef *(indicates F)*

Repeat Signs

Da Capo From the beginning; return to the top of the music (abbreviated *D.C.*).

Dal Segno Go back to the section marked with the sign (abbreviated *D.S.*).

D.S. sign: 𝄋

Coda A short passage which formally ends a piece.

Coda sign: ⊕

Other Signs and Terms

Ottava Up or down an octave (abbreviated *8va*).

written:

played:

8va - - - - - - - - - ⌐

A Tempo Return to the original tempo.

Accelerando Gradually becoming faster (abbreviated *accel.*).

Fermata Hold the note longer than its written value, often at the discretion of the conductor.

Fermata sign: 𝄐

Segue Move immediately to the next section or piece without a pause.

Transpose To play the part in a key other than the one in which it is written.

Tacit Rest; lay out.

Below is an example of a bass part using the symbols that we have discussed.

The above example would run as follows:

Intro   8 bars
Chorus   16 bars
Interlude   8 bars
D.S. (repeat Chorus) 16 bars
D.C. (repeat Intro) 8 bars
Coda

Letters may also be used to mark the sections of a piece. For example:

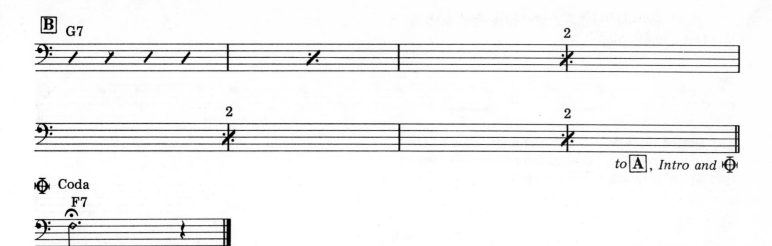

to **A**, Intro and ⊕

This example would run as follows:

Intro	8 bars
A	16 bars
B	8 bars
A	16 bars
Intro	8 bars
Coda	

Counting Rhythms

In a bar of $\frac{4}{4}$, there are eight eighth-notes. Dividing the bar into two equal parts, with an imaginary middle line, assists in accurately locating the downbeats and upbeats. For example:

So, the following rhythmic figure

4 eighths + 4 eighths

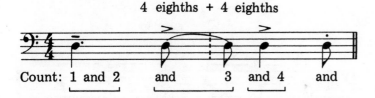

should *not* be written like this:

5 eighths + 3 eighths

An exception to this would be the following figure:

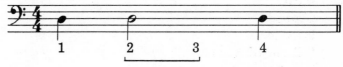

In addition, the notation used in this example

is better than this:

By not putting beams across the middle of the bar, the main beat is more apparent.

Tied notes are another way of making a rhythmic idea better understood.

Dotted rhythms can be better understood by taking a comparable, more easily comprehendible, larger rhythm and reducing it. For example:

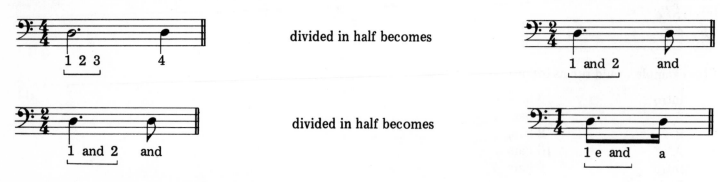

divided in half becomes

divided in half becomes

Sixteenth notes are counted like this:

So the following rhythmic figure would be counted like this:

A *triplet* sign indicates that the designated group of three notes is to be played within the same time value normally taken up by a group of two of the same type of note. The following are quarter-note triplets.

These are eighth-note triplets.

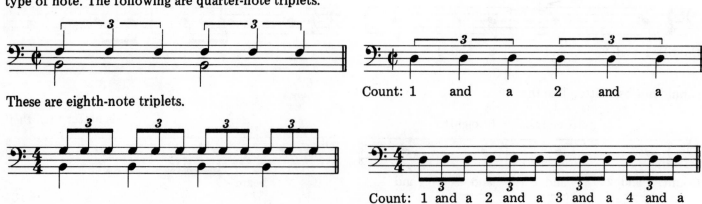

Note that eighth notes in rock are "felt"—and thus played—differently than they are in jazz. The following example would be played as it is written in a rock situation.

However, in a jazz situation it would be played like this:

In other words, the difference between rock and jazz performances of straight eighth-notes is:

Syncopation is the shift of accent from the normally accented *beat* to the normally unaccented *offbeat* ("and" beats). The goal of tension and release in rhythmic improvisation can best be achieved by maintaining a balance of syncopation versus normal accent-patterns.

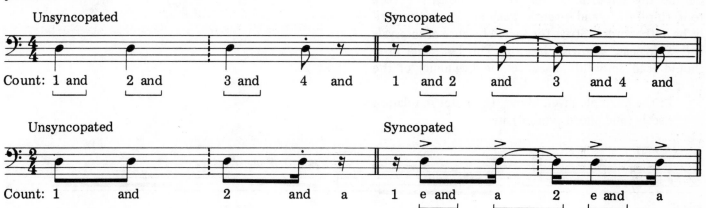

Making Up a Bass Figure

Frequently, the bassist in a group is asked to make up a bass *riff*, or *ostinato* (definition: a short melodic phrase or figure persistently repeated by the same instrument). Usually this is done spontaneously and is based on the feel of the music in question.

This section deals with a practical way to gain ability in this area. Since it's usually not possible to sit down and figure out a bass riff on a piece of paper in a playing situation, this exercise provides a good opportunity to explore this process on your own. It is a useful way to come up with interesting rhythmic lines for bass figures and can be used in all styles and in various time signatures.

Exercise in Bass Figures

Notice that there are sixteen eighth-notes in two measures of $\frac{4}{4}$.

By adding up combinations of numbers *1*, *2*, and *3*, to equal 16, some interesting syncopated rhythms can occur. Select the numbers at random and put them in various combinations. Avoid using all equal numbers as no syncopation will occur.

Using the above rhythmic line in combination with the following chord scale

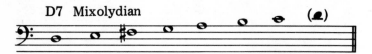

a bass line could be made as follows:

When choosing the melodic shape of the figure, aim to outline the important notes of the chord; i. e., the root, third, fifth, and seventh. They need not necessarily be in that order. Strive for a good balance of intervals and a logical, stepwise motion. The last tone used should lead smoothly back to the beginning of the figure.

In the example given above, the notes in relation to the scale (and chord symbol) are:

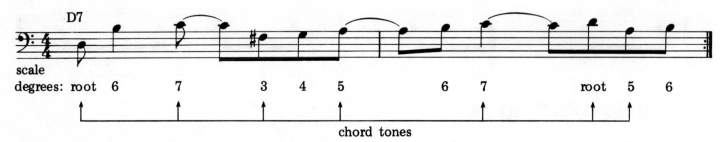

Here is an example of the same rhythmic line and chord scale, but using wider intervals.

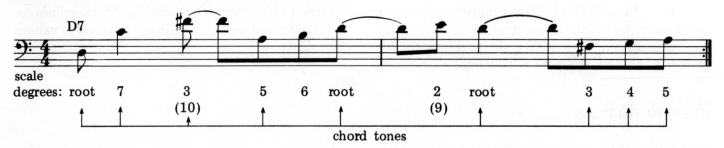

To put in rests, select numbers at random and circle them. For example:

68

A new bass figure could be as follows:

You can get additional rhythmic figures by taking your original idea and writing it out backwards. For example:

Original:

Backwards:

These can be strung together to make one four-bar figure.

Applying this "numbers game" to sixteenth notes increases rhythmic activity since there are thirty-two sixteenth notes in two measures.

The numbers *1*, *2*, *3*, *4*, and *5*, can be used to create syncopation.

By putting the above rhythmic figure together with the scale below

C-7 Dorian

one gets the following figure:

Fast rock
C-7

Here is the same basic pattern, but with the insertion
of rests.

Fast rock

By using sixteenth notes, you can create exercises
that flow melodically and use more than one chord
scale. Here is an example of two chords within one
figure.

Four chords within one figure:

Three chords within one figure:

To get familiar with the numbers game, write out
several rhythmic lines using various combinations of
numbers and apply them to chord scales. Start with
eighth-notes and as you become fluent, move to sixteenth notes. Play each example and see how your
choice of notes in the figure feels, and how it might be
improved. The aim is to create a musically interesting
bass figure for any type of musical situation, and ulti-
mately to have the ability to do this spontaneously.

This exercise can be a lot of fun and will greatly
increase your reading skills as well as develop your ear
for putting together notes that sound good. It's a great
game—enjoy it!

Study Assignment—Bass Figures

Using the music on the preceding pages as an example, make up three different bass figures based on the following rhythms; then write them out and play them.

Bass Figures in Odd Time Signatures

The majority of pop and jazz composition are written in $\frac{4}{4}$ or *common time*, and the bulk of the music that a bassist encounters is in this meter. For this reason many musicians seem to resist the fun and challenge that can be found in playing with *odd time signatures*. While it's unlikely that music written in unusual rhythms will ever become popular, it is well worth the time and effort to experiment with it, if only for the benefits gained by going against deeply ingrained mechanical habits of thought, and allowing oneself to realize a new way of looking at things.

Music in odd time signatures has been in existence for a very long time. Indian classical musicians come immediately to mind as being the most proficient and skilled when dealing with these meters. By listening to recordings of Indian master musicians, one can gain a good insight into their ingenious handling of unusual rhythms. These recordings can be found in most large record stores. *The Inner Mounting Flame*, by the Mahavishnu Orchestra contains many examples of odd time signatures within the context of jazz/fusion music.

Below is the basic eighth-note count in $\frac{5}{4}$.

However, the measure can be subdivided in several other ways.

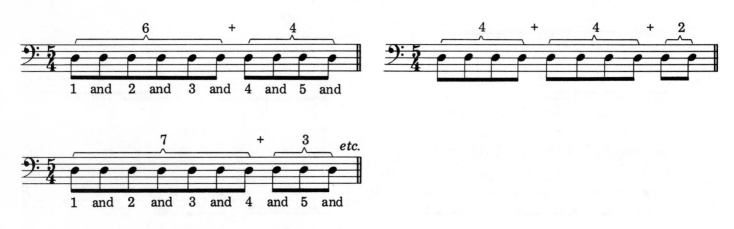

As in the previous chapter, the use of sixteenth notes offers many other variations.

Go through the following examples of creating bass figures in various time signatures step by step.

$\frac{5}{4}$ Time

Step One—Write out a rhythm. Carefully tap, and count it out.

Step Two—Select a scale.

G-7 Dorian

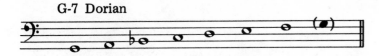

Step Three—Take the notes found in the scale that you have selected and put them into your basic rhythmic figure (Step One).

Medium
G-7

Step Four—Play this figure on the bass, aiming for rhythmic accuracy and an even tone.

7/4 Time

Step One—

Step Two—

E-7 Diatonic Pentatonic (G: 4th inversion)

Step Three—

Slow
E-7

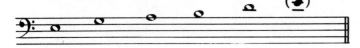

Play through the above figure (Step Four). Listen to the contrast in sound when a different chord scale is plugged into the same rhythm.

Bb 7 Lydian

Medium
Bb 7

$\frac{9}{4}$ Time

Step One—

Step Two—

D-7 Diatonic Pentatonic (F: 3rd inversion)

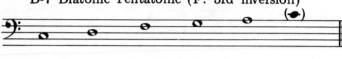

Step Three—

Fast

D-7

$\frac{11}{8}$ Time

Step One—

Step Two—

F7 Altered

root   ♭9   ♯9   3   ♭5   ♭13   ♭7

Step Three—

F7 Altered

Slow

Notice in the following examples how the rhythmic activity is increased by using sixteenth notes.

Medium rock

F♯ -7 Dorian

1   2   3   4   5   6   7

Slow rock

B-7 Pentatonic

1   2   3   4   5

Study Assignment—Odd Times

1. Following the example of the preceding pages, write three figures using each of the following rhythms. Try three different scales for each one, then play them.

2. Make up some odd-time-signature rhythms of your own choice and add chord scales. You may want to try the numbers game to come up with ideas.

Making a Walking Bass Line

The function of the bass in rock and fusion music is for the most part based on repeated figures of percussive riffs. In jazz the role is somewhat different as the principal function consists of providing a walking bass line. This style of playing evolved over the years and was developed by many fine acoustic bassists.

To gain a good insight into this concept, the student is urged to listen closely to some of the bassists listed at the end of this book and find out the various ways a walking bass line can be approached. The walking bass line is a constant melodic line that is played through the composition and provides an outline of the chord changes. It is over this line that the soloists or ensemble perform. The main qualities to strive for are (a) a stable and flowing rhythm, (b) a good sound, (c) smooth lines that also connect with the chords, and (d) a solid support of the soloist or group by being flexible and listening constantly.

Although the function of the walking bass line is traditionally the territory of the acoustic bass, it is quite common currently for the electric bass guitar to also fill this role. Here are some points to observe when playing a walking line on the electric bass:

1. Set the volume lower than it is usually used when playing rock. Try to match the volume of the other instruments in the rhythm section.

2. Set the tone for a nice fat sound without too much treble.

3. Play quarter notes longer, striving for a continuous flow of sound from note to note.

4. Be physically comfortable when you are playing. Jazz pieces can go on for a long time and the bassist must play throughout. Sitting on a stool or comfortable chair can help you to be relaxed.

Open-String Rhythm Studies

Play through the following exercises using a metronome. You are aiming for a stable and flowing rhythm. The exercises progress from one to two, and finally to three and four strings.

Three and Four Strings

Study Assignment—Blues Lines

Play through the following blues bass line set to a relatively standard progression. Once you have mastered it, make up your own chord progression and create a walking line to go with it.

D.C.

Blues Lines with Embellishments

The following bass line uses the same chord progression as above, only it has been embellished rhythmically and melodically to add interest.

Study Assignment—Blues Lines with Embellishments

When playing blues, the following scales can be used on any Dominant 7th chord: Lydian, Mixolydian, Altered, and Whole Tone.

1. Make a walking bass line (without embellishments) through the chords in the following 12-bar blues.

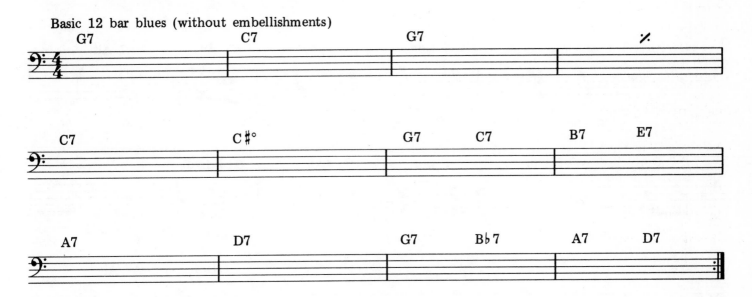

Once you have written out the line and played it, ask yourself if each bar flows smoothly into the next.

2. Take the line that you wrote out above and add embellishments. Do not add too many, or they will interfere with the flow.

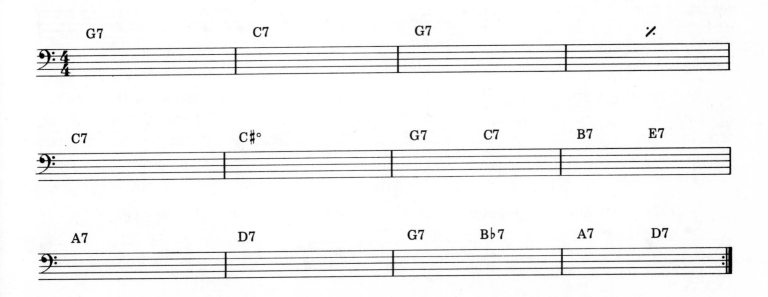

Minor Blues Lines

The following example is of a walking bass line in a minor key.

Study Assignment— Minor Blues Lines

Write out a walking bass line through these minor blues changes.

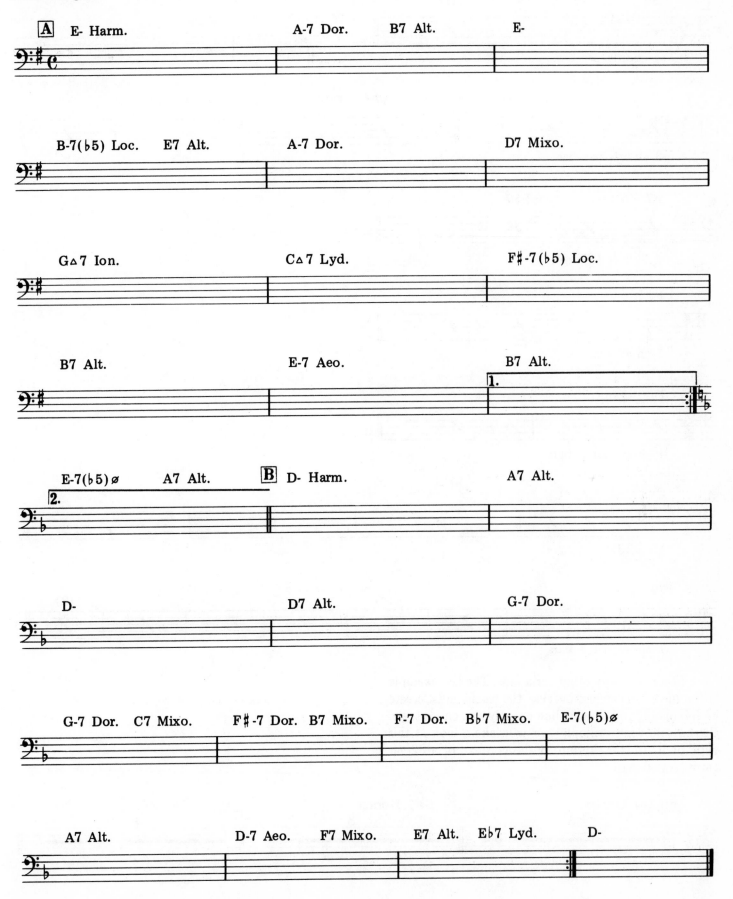

Harmonic Rhythm

Harmonic rhythm refers to the duration of a given chord. Look at the following series of examples.

1.
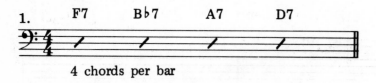

4 chords per bar

2.

3 chords per bar

3.
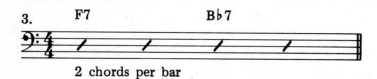

2 chords per bar

4.
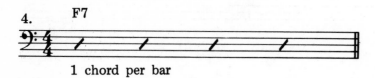

1 chord per bar

5.
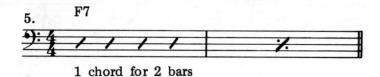

1 chord for 2 bars

6.

1 chord for 4 bars

7.
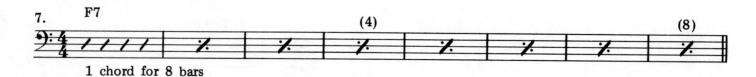

1 chord for 8 bars

There are many other variations. The last example is the most challenging because the bassist must create an interesting and flowing line on only one chord scale. In the following example, we will take a look at this type of harmonic rhythm in the context of a 32-bar form (A A B A).

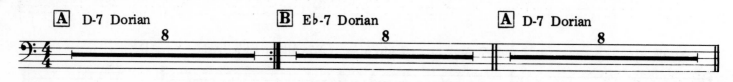

84

In order to approach the chart given above, you must first determine the chord scales for both the A and B sections.

You can now create a bass line. Play through the following to get a good feel of this particular kind of harmonic rhythm. Continue by making up your own line from the correct chord scales.

D.C. (Back to A)

Play a walking bass line through these changes:

D.C.

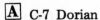  

Chromatic Tones

Chromatic tones are the notes found within the octave not included in the chord scale. For example, in C Major, the notes with an asterisk are chromatics:

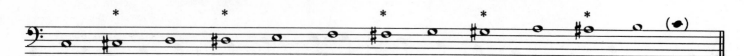

Chromatic tones that are not in the chord scale of the moment may be used as passing tones in walking bass lines, or solos. In the following example they are again indicated by an asterisk.

Study Assignment—
Harmonic Rhythms

1. Play through the following example as it is written, then begin to make up your own lines using the same chord progression.

2. Make a walking bass line through these chords:

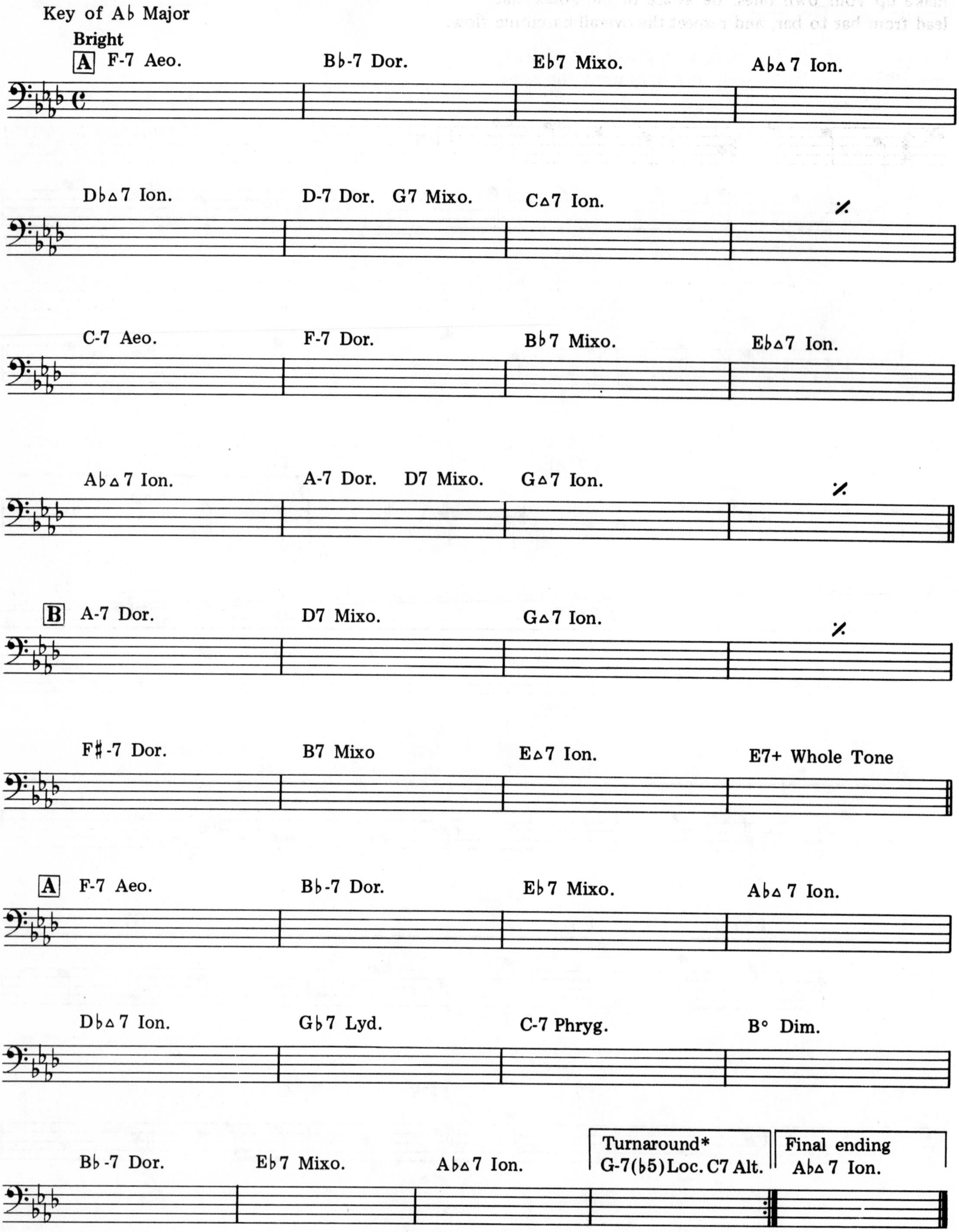

Key of Ab Major

Bright

[A] F-7 Aeo.　　　　Bb-7 Dor.　　　　Eb7 Mixo.　　　　AbΔ7 Ion.

DbΔ7 Ion.　　　　D-7 Dor.　G7 Mixo.　　　CΔ7 Ion.　　　　 ⁒

C-7 Aeo.　　　　F-7 Dor.　　　　Bb7 Mixo.　　　　EbΔ7 Ion.

AbΔ7 Ion.　　　　A-7 Dor.　D7 Mixo.　　　GΔ7 Ion.　　　　 ⁒

[B] A-7 Dor.　　　　D7 Mixo.　　　　GΔ7 Ion.　　　　 ⁒

F♯-7 Dor.　　　　B7 Mixo　　　　EΔ7 Ion.　　　　E7+ Whole Tone

[A] F-7 Aeo.　　　　Bb-7 Dor.　　　　Eb7 Mixo.　　　　AbΔ7 Ion.

DbΔ7 Ion.　　　　Gb7 Lyd.　　　　C-7 Phryg.　　　　B° Dim.

Bb-7 Dor.　　　　Eb7 Mixo.　　　　AbΔ7 Ion.　　　Turnaround*　│　Final ending
　　　　　　　　　　　　　　　　　　　　　　　　　　　G-7(b5)Loc. C7 Alt.　│　AbΔ7 Ion.

Turnaround: Chords leading back to the beginning.

3. Play the following line as written, then begin to
make up your own lines. Be aware of the notes that
lead from bar to bar, and respect the overall harmonic flow.

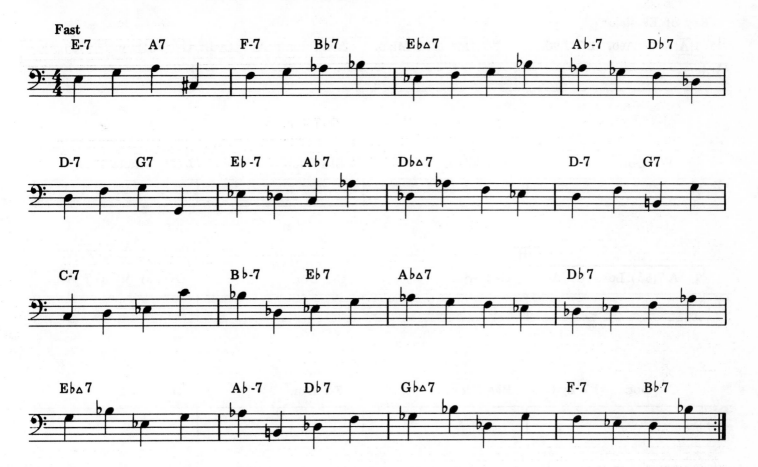

4. Make a walking bass line through these chords:

Key of Eb Major

[A] C-7 Aeo. Gb7 Lyd.   F-7 Dor. Bb7 Mixo.   Eb△7 Ion. Ab7 Lyd.   G-7(b5) Loc. C7(b9) Alt.

F-7 Dor.   Bb7 Mixo.   Eb△7 Ion.   1. G7+ Whole Tone

[B]
2. A-7(b5) Loc. D7 Alt.   G- Harm.   C-7 Dor.   D7(b9) Alt. G-7 Aeo.

C-7 Dor. F7 Lyd.   Bb△7 Ion.   F-7 Dor.   D-7(b5) Loc.

G7+ Whole Tone   [A] C-7 Aeo. Gb7 Lyd.   F-7 Dor. Bb7 Mixo.   Eb△7 Ion. Ab7 Lyd.

G-7(b5) C7(b9)
Loc.   Alt.   F-7 Dor.   Bb7 Mixo.   Eb△7 Ion.   ⁒

5. Play through this line as it's written a few times,
then begin making your own on these changes:

6. Make a walking bass line through these chords:

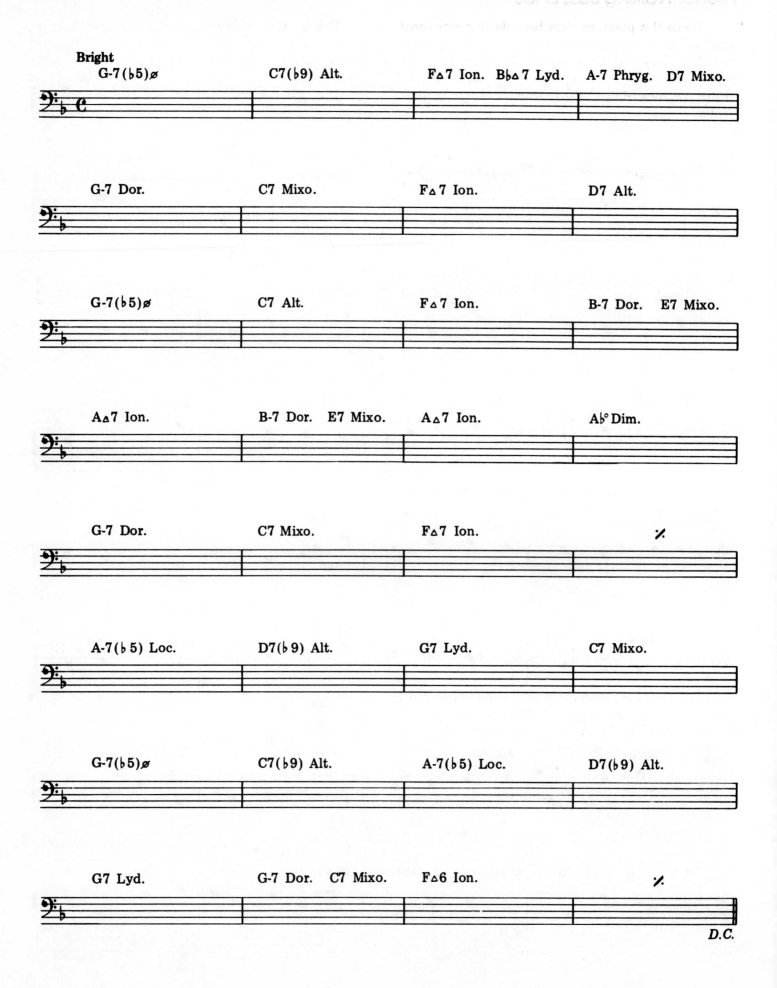

Bright

G-7(♭5)ø — C7(♭9) Alt. — F△7 Ion. B♭△7 Lyd. A-7 Phryg. D7 Mixo.

G-7 Dor. — C7 Mixo. — F△7 Ion. — D7 Alt.

G-7(♭5)ø — C7 Alt. — F△7 Ion. — B-7 Dor. E7 Mixo.

A△7 Ion. — B-7 Dor. E7 Mixo. — A△7 Ion. — A♭° Dim.

G-7 Dor. — C7 Mixo. — F△7 Ion. — %

A-7(♭5) Loc. — D7(♭9) Alt. — G7 Lyd. — C7 Mixo.

G-7(♭5)ø — C7(♭9) Alt. — A-7(♭5) Loc. — D7(♭9) Alt.

G7 Lyd. — G-7 Dor. C7 Mixo. — F△6 Ion. — %

D.C.

Atonal Walking Bass Lines

Up to this point we have been dealing with *tonal* applications of chord scales when creating a walking bass line. However, there are certain styles of music where the bassist must improvise bass lines that are atonal; i.e., not related to any common chords or tonic center.

This is a very challenging area as the object here is to not outline recognizable harmonies and at the same time to remain musical. In this next section we will take a look at a way to approach this.

The following *tone row* will be used as the basis for an atonal line:

A tone row is made from the twelve tones of the chromatic scale:

There are several possible permutations of the row. One is through *inversion*, the reversal of the direction of the intervals.

Here is the original row in *retrograde* (backwards);

and the *retrograde inversion:*

The following example is of a walking line using the original row and its permutations in sequence with an interesting rhythm added. Play it through as it's written, then make up some of your own lines based on the tone row and its permutations.

Below is an example of the row used as an ostinato line.

Rhythmic outline:

Medium

Study Assignment— Walking Bass Lines

1. Find some standard or jazz composition. Write out the chord progressions and figure out the correct chord scale for each chord. Make up some walking lines through these changes.

2. Select a recording by one of the bassists listed at the end of this book and write out the bass line to a composition that he plays on. Then play along with the record while reading the written line. This will give you a good insight into the way a line relates to the music of the group. It is also very good ear training. Pick something simple at first, something that you can handle easily.

3. Make up some chord progressions of your own and walk a line through them.

About Soloing

One of the traditional functions of the acoustic bassist in jazz is the ability to improvise a solo on the chords or modes of a composition. This is the area in which a bassist can really distinguish himself. Indeed, it is a most challenging task, for it is where one's total musical wares are on display.

Soloing on the electric bass is a relatively recent phenomenon and only a handful of players have risen to the challenge. It is largely a matter of concept. By opening one's imagination to *all* types of music—especially the solos of guitarists, tenor saxophonists, pianists, etc.—and listening to their melodic interpretations and phrasing ideas, one can begin to duplicate and develop a true improvisational style. Think of a solo as a conversation; or a statement about thoughts and feelings. Don't limit yourself to thinking within the confines of the bass but rather imagine you are singing a song. It can be pretty, happy, sad, nasty—*any* emotion you want it to be at that particular time. The main thing is to communicate, and to do so *through* your music.

By listening closely to all types of music—jazz, pop, classical, Indian, Brazilian, country, Latin, etc.—you can begin to see that the scope of musical ideas is infinite and that you can draw your inspiration and concept from many sources.

A primary characteristic of the skilled soloist is the ability to develop an idea and logically build it until it reaches its conclusion. While a facile technique is admirable, speed in and of itself is not the only criterion of skill for a soloist. A good example of a soloist who uses an economy of notes is Miles Davis. Following a solo of his, note by note from the beginning, is a good way to gain insight into saying a lot

with very little. On the other hand, a different approach to soloing can be found in the work of the late saxophonist, John Coltrane, who developed a remarkable technique and used it most beautifully to express himself.

In the following chapter, we will take a look at some ways to approach a solo. This is where all of the preceding concepts and information—chord scales, intervals, triads, pentatonics, etc.—will be drawn upon.

Developing an Idea

Regardless of the style of music that one intends to improvise, the substance or content of a well-made solo is based on ideas and their development. A musical idea can be a short phrase, or a long one based on the scale of the moment. It can even be an abstraction outside of the scale. For our purposes here, we will stick to phrases based on the scale of the moment, as one must first learn the basics before breaking the rules. The well-developed jazz soloist has usually done his homework in these basics, and has reached a level of creativity that is spontaneous; with ideas flowing freely one to another.

Running up and down scales, no matter how facile and correct it may be, does not a solo make. The soloist must be able to communicate to the listener, to sing through the instrument, and to make a statement that can be understood and possibly duplicated by others. Listen to solos on all instruments in all types of music and observe how ideas are developed. It is really very simple: Learn the material (scales, intervals, rhythms, etc.), apply them, and keep on doing it until it sounds good.

Developing an Idea on a Minor Blues

Basic idea

Below are some examples of how this basic idea can be explored and developed. The soloist is offered a number of options in his approach.

95

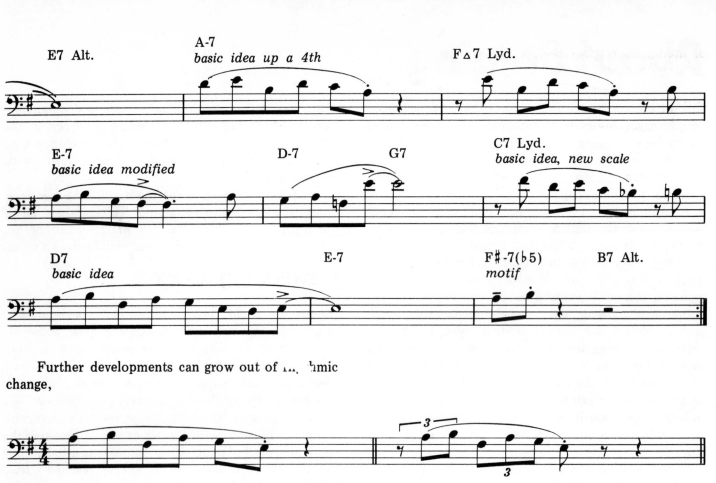

Further developments can grow out of rhythmic change,

an inversion of the basic idea,

paring it down to motifs,

using sequences,

or altering the original melodic concept.

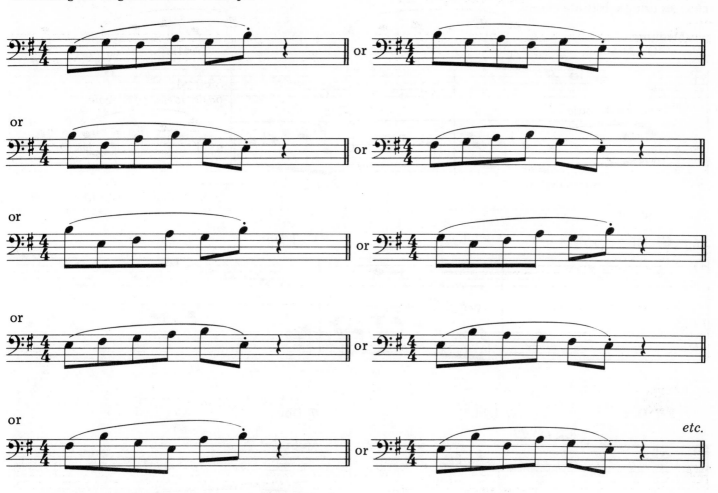

Below is an example of the use of pentatonics in developing an idea.

The following is an example of soloing on blues changes using substitute chords.

* Intervals above the octave:

Exercises on Soloing

1. Before making a solo on these blues changes, play a walking line on the chord scales until you are completely familiar with the overall harmonic flow.

Key of F Major

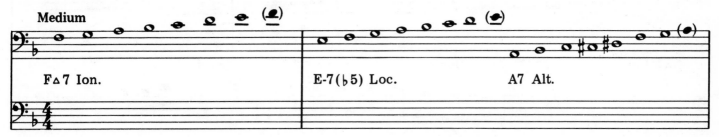

Medium

F△7 Ion.   E-7(♭5) Loc.   A7 Alt.

D-7 Aeo.   D♭7 Lyd.   C-7 Dor.   F7 Mixo.

B♭△7 Ion.   B♭-7 Dor.   E♭7 Mixo.   A♭△7 Ion.

D♭△7 Ion.   G-7 Dor.   C7 Mixo.   B♭7 Lyd.

A7 Lyd.   D7 Lyd.   G7 Lyd.   C7 Lyd.

2. **Play through this exercise as written; then make up your own solo.**

3. **Play through this solo as written; then make up your own solo on these modal changes.**

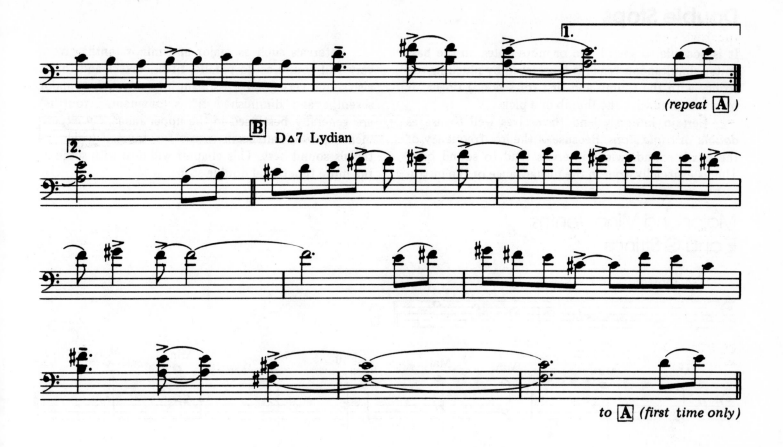

(repeat **A**)

B D△7 Lydian

to **A** (first time only)

Study Assignment—Solos

1. Find some standard jazz compositions and write out the chord progressions. Figure out the chord scales. First play a walking line through the changes; then begin to make up a solo based on these chords.

2. Make up some chord progressions of your own and use them to solo on.

3. Write a number of short melodic ideas and develop them into a full length bass solo. Use some of the various idea development suggestions: inversion, rhythmic changes, etc.

Double Stops

It is possible to sound two or more notes on the bass guitar simultaneously. This is achieved by plucking the strings with the thumb and first (or second) finger; or by strumming with the thumb or a pick.

Certain intervals lend themselves well to use as *double* or *triple stops*. Because of the low frequency of the bass's sound, wider intervals tend to sound best. This is especially true in the higher range of the instrument.

Intervals such as major and minor tenths give a very full sound, as do parallel fifths. Sixths and thirds also sound very good. Dissonant intervals such as major sevenths and diminished fifths (augmented fourths) are generally best used in the upper range. By experimenting, you can begin to see for yourself which intervals sound best. This chapter will deal with some of the more functional double stops.

Major and Minor Tenths: E and G Strings

Pluck with thumb and first finger

102

Note that the Whole-Tone scale yields major tenths only:

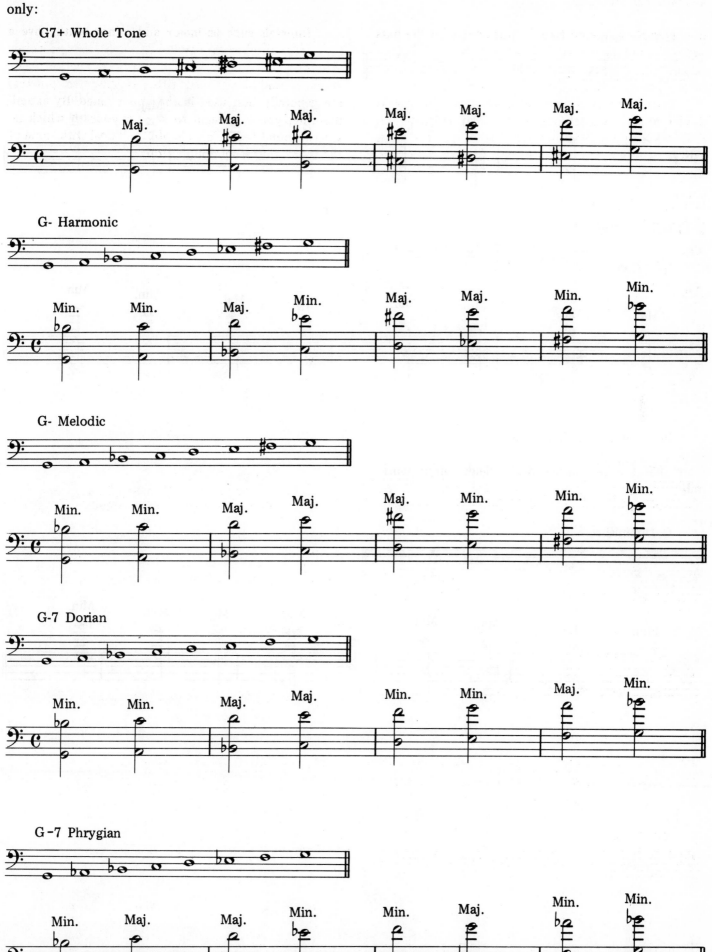

103

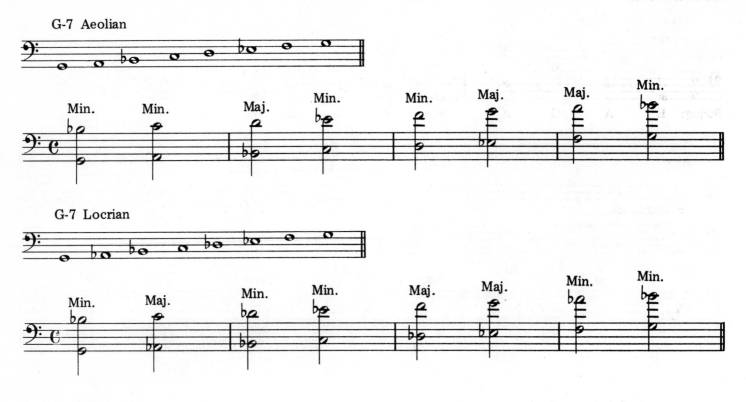

Note that the Diminished scale yields minor tenths only:

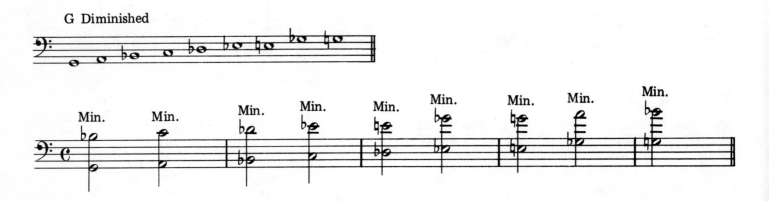

The following is an exercise in playing tenths with
the fifth added.

Bass Lines Using Tenths

The *samba*, along with the *bossa nova*, is one of the Brazilian rhythms which has become a standard part of the repertoire of many jazz groups. It is a great rhythm to play, and the most important part of a bassist's role in this music is the groove he gets into with the percussion section. It is best felt in $\frac{2}{2}$ time (¢, or cut time) as the tempo is usually fairly bright.

The best way to familiarize yourself with this music is to listen to records of artists who feature it. Milton Nascimento, Airto, or Chick Corea on *Light as a Feather* are some good examples. Listening to and playing along with their music will give you a good insight as to what a bassist needs to do in order to function best within these rhythms.

106

Other Intervals

The following are examples of different intervals combined.

tenths and sevenths:

thirds and sixths:

chorale style:

Unaccompanied
Bass Guitar Solo

The following composition is an example of a way to
use various intervals in a bass guitar solo.

City and Eastern Blues

Rick Laird

Conclusion

The material offered in this book has been set forth
with one basic purpose: To offer the bassist interested
in learning about improvisation some insight into the
various ways it can be approached. Many of the subjects covered could fill an entire book on their own.
Therefore, my intention has been to provide enough
data to stimulate the student into pursuing each of
these areas, and to encourage him to begin to formu-
late an individual way of applying the principles involved to actual playing situations.

Much improvement in ability can be gained by
studying textbooks, but by far the most important
tool for speeding up the process is strong intention,
and the motivation and discipline to persist on a
chosen course of action. It need not take ten years to
be an excellent bassist—though some may try to tell
you this. It takes as long as it takes for you to get a
grasp of the basics and learn to apply them. I hope
this book has taken some of the mystery out of
them for you, while you pursue your goals. Have fun!

Rick Laird

Bibliography

Bach, J. S. *371 Chorales*. New York: Associated Music Publishers, Inc. (For harmonic study.)

Bach, J. S. *Two-Part Inventions*. New York: Schirmer Books. (For sight-reading practice.)

Brown, Ray. *Ray Brown Bass Method*. Ray Brown Publishing.

Coker, Jerry. *Improvising Jazz*. Englewood Cliffs, NJ: Prentice-Hall, Inc.

Hindemith, Paul. *Elementary Training for Musicians*. London: Schott & Co., Ltd.

Nanny, Eduoard. *Complete Method for Bass, Books I and II*. Paris: Leduc Publishing.

Persichetti, Vincent. *Twentieth Century Harmony*. New York: W. W. Norton & Company, Inc.

Reid, Rufus. *The Evolving Bassist*. Lebanon, IN: Studio P/R, Inc.

Slonimsky, Nicholas. *Thesaurus of Scales and Melodic Patterns*. New York: Charles Scribner's Sons.

Appendix: Bassists to Listen To

This list contains some of the key figures who have contributed, and continue to contribute, to the evolution of jazz bass in contemporary music. There are many, many others who have made valuable contributions and have not been included. However, this list will provide a well-rounded picture of some of the ways to approach the art of bass playing.

The dates given do not represent the total output of these artists. Rather, they define specific periods as listening examples.

Acoustic Bassists

Jimmy Blanton*	Duke Ellington Band 1930-40s
Oscar Pettiford*	Various 1945-55
Ray Brown	Oscar Peterson Trio 1955-65
Charles Mingus*	Leader 1955-79
Percy Heath	Modern Jazz Quartet 1955-75
Paul Chambers*	Miles Davis 1955-62
Ron Carter	Miles Davis 1964-68
Richard Davis	Thad Jones/Mel Lewis Orchestra 1965-70
Scott La Faro*	Bill Evans Trio 1959-62
Eddie Gomez	Bill Evans Trio 1968-77

Other Bassists

Jaco Pastorius	*Weather Report* Columbia PC-30661 *Jaco Pastorius* Epic PE-33949
Stanley Clarke	*Return to Forever* ECM 1022 *Light as a Feather* Polydor 5525 with Chick Corea
Eberhard Weber	*Colors of Chloe* ECM 1042
Dave Holland	*Conference of the Birds* ECM 1027
Mike Richmond	*Dream Waves* Inner City 1065
Will Lee	*Brecker Brothers* Arista 4037
Niels Henning-Orsted-Pederson	Various albums with Oscar Peterson on Pablo Records
Sam Jones	Various albums with Cannonball Adderley on Riverside Records
Jack Bruce	Various albums with Cream on RSO Records
Buster Williams	*Piccolo* Milestone 55004 with Ron Carter
Steve Swallow	Various albums with Gary Burton on ECM Records
Rick Laird	*The Inner Mounting Flame* Columbia PC-31067 *Birds of Fire* Columbia PC-31996 *Between Nothingness and Eternity* Columbia C-32766 with the Mahavishnu Orchestra *Still on the Planet* Muse 5063 with Eddie Jefferson *New York Afternoon* Muse 5119 with Richie Cole *Brief Encounter* Muse 5154 with Eddie Daniels *Rick Laird—Soft Focus* Timeless-Muse TI 308 featuring Joe Henderson

*deceased